BILLYBALL

BILLYBALL

◎◎◎◎

Billy Martin
WITH
Phil Pepe

DOUBLEDAY & COMPANY, INC.
GARDEN CITY, NEW YORK
1987

Library of Congress Cataloging-in-Publication Data
Martin, Billy, 1928–
    Billyball.
    1. Baseball—United States—Miscellanea.   I. Pepe,
Phil.   II. Title.
GV863.A1M36   1987   796.357'0973   86-29057
ISBN: 0-385-23491-0.

This book is dedicated to two men who guided me, helped me, counseled me and befriended me—Red Adams, trainer for the Oakland Oaks in the Pacific Coast League, who helped get my baseball career started, and Pete Sheehy, clubhouse man for the New York Yankees, who helped me keep my baseball career going and helped me keep things in their proper perspective.

—Billy Martin

BILLYBALL

1

Why am I doing another book? That's a good question and I'll try to answer it. For one thing, it has been almost seven years since my last book was published and, obviously, a lot has happened to me in seven years that you might want to get caught up on. For another, the emphasis of this book is somewhat different than the last one.

I'm hoping this book can tell you more about Billy Martin the manager, in addition to Billy Martin the man. I would like this to be a kind of a Manual of Managing, if you will, outlining my approach to managing, my technique as a manager, how I go about the job of managing a baseball team.

The title *BillyBall* comes from a slogan that

was used by an Oakland sportswriter, Ralph Wiley, to describe the style of play that my Oakland A's were using in the 1981 season. There was nothing different about that style that I hadn't used in the four other cities I managed—good, hard, aggressive baseball; forcing the other team into making mistakes; steal, hit-and-run, take the extra base. If BillyBall is not new or unique, it is uniquely Billy Martin. You can always identify a Billy Martin team by its aggressiveness.

And as the title implies, this book is intended to tell you something about my style of baseball.

Baseball is the greatest game ever invented, and one of the things that make it great is that it can be as simple, or as complex, as you want it to be. Everybody and anybody with a television set or the price of a ticket can be an expert on baseball. Or think he's an expert.

It doesn't take a genius to know when to bunt, when to hit-and-run, when to bring in a new pitcher. That's the charm of baseball for the average fan. But things are not always that simple.

No fan, or sportswriter, or broadcaster, or scout, or general manager, or owner, for that matter, knows as much about the team on the field, and the individuals who make up that team, as the manager. Sometimes, a move that seems so obvious to the fan in the stands, or sitting in his living room, is not that obvious to the manager. There are reasons he does certain things, or does not do certain things.

The fan might think it's obvious that the manager should bring in his best relief pitcher in a certain critical situation. But what the fan might not know is that the relief pitcher has pitched four consecutive days, or warmed up five or six straight days, and has told the manager before the game that his arm is tired. The manager knows he can't use his relief pitcher, let's say it's Dave Righetti, but he's not going to tell the press Righetti is unavailable, because he doesn't want the other manager to find out. Let the other manager think he might have to face Righetti. It might force him to make a move he might not otherwise make.

There are other things I will discuss in the pages that follow—such as why I hit-and-run on a certain count, against a certain pitcher, with a certain hitter. Every move I make as a manager has a reason. Just as there is a reason for every move I don't make.

Baseball has been my life. It's the thing I know best and the thing I have done best. I have been a major league player—not a Hall of Famer, but a pretty successful player, especially in World Series competition. And I have been a successful manager. I think I have something I can share with the fans—my knowledge of the game.

Things don't just happen by accident on the field. They usually happen for a reason. I feel I have prepared for my job of managing with the most thorough education I could get. Nothing ever came easy for me as a player. I had limited ability and I had to do the little things to make myself a more valuable player; those little things that make the difference between winning and losing. And it was this determination to make myself a better and more valuable player that taught me so much about the game.

As a second baseman, I feel I had an advantage for my future career of manager. Middle infielders—shortstops and second basemen—usually make the best managers because they are more involved in the game in more ways than players at any other positions.

I have managed in the minor leagues, which I feel is essential, and I have coached third base and scouted. I have had a well-rounded baseball education. And I have had some great teachers. We're all the products of our experience, and the experience of playing for such outstanding managers as Casey Stengel, Charlie Dressen and Freddy Hutchinson has helped me become a successful manager.

There is more to managing than filling out the lineup card and bringing in a new pitcher. There are relationships with the players, front office relationships, evaluating talent, knowing human nature, knowing when to push a team and when to back off. All of these facets will be discussed in the following pages.

To what do I attribute my success as a manager? So many things. My training, for one. Also, I am a stickler for detail. I come to a game well prepared to do my job. I try to stay two or three batters, sometimes two or three innings, ahead. If it's the fourth inning, I might be thinking of a move I can make in the seventh inning.

"Guidry looks like he doesn't have good stuff, I'd better get my bullpen ready. . . . Weaver has already used two of his right-handed hitters to pinch-hit, trying to get back in the game. . . . I'll get another left-handed pitcher ready because there aren't many moves Weaver can make. . . ."

I drive my players and my coaches hard, especially in spring training. I want them to do things over and over so that they come automatically.

It has been said that a good manager can win anywhere from eight to twelve games a year for his team. That might not seem like much, but when you consider that most pennants are won by from three to eight games, a manager can make the Hall of Fame if he can win eight to twelve games a year for his team.

In this book, I intend to discuss managerial strategy, to give you an idea how Billy Martin thinks, how he goes about the business of managing a baseball team. I will grade other managers, I'll discuss front office relationships and owners I have worked for, I'll talk about the state of the game, what I see as baseball's major problems and what suggestions I have to solve those problems. I'll talk about the people I have met, the friends I have made.

And I'll present Billy Martin's All-Stars, made up of players I played with and against, managed and managed against.

Baseball has been my life for forty years. It's the only job I have ever had. I have done what I have wanted to do with my life and, in that respect, I consider myself very fortunate and I consider my life a success. This does not mean that I have been perfect or that my life has been perfect. There are some things I would change if I could.

I regret that I have not lived a stable and secure existence. I left home when I was eighteen to play baseball and I have never really had a permanent home since then. I regret that. I have had three marriages that failed and I regret that, too. I'm not going to get into why those marriages failed or who was at fault. I am willing to accept my share of the blame for those failures. I regret, too, that I didn't spend as much time with my family, and with my two children, as I would have liked.

I regret that, but I'm not apologizing for it. I made my bed and I'll sleep in it. I wanted to be a baseball player for as far back as I can remember. Then, once I started managing, I was bitten by the bug and I wanted to be the best manager I could be. I played for the New York Yankees and I managed the New York Yankees and that's like a baritone singing at La Scala or an artist having one of his paintings hanging in the Louvre.

Being a player and a manager for the New York Yankees, the greatest team in sports, has been a thrill and a privilege that I will never regret, even though it didn't always turn out the way I hoped it would.

Nevertheless, I did the things I wanted to do and I did them to the best of my ability, and for that, there are no regrets and no apologies. Even with all the sacrifices I have had to make, all the things I have had to miss, all the owners who have fired me, it's been a great life. Very few people get to work at a job they love, and I'm one of them.

You want to talk about pride? Let me tell you about Sunday, August 10, 1986. Billy Martin Day at Yankee Stadium, a day I'll never forget. It was the greatest day of my life. Nothing will ever top it. Nothing possibly could.

It wasn't just because they retired my No. 1 or because they dedicated a plaque to me which will stand next to the monuments in center field, right next to Babe Ruth, Lou Gehrig, Joe DiMaggio, Casey Stengel, Mickey Mantle and other Yankees greats. It wasn't because of all the wonderful gifts I received from so many thoughtful people.

No, what made this day so special was the love and warmth I felt coming down from the stands. And what made it so extra special was that my mother was there to witness it all.

We were standing there, lined up at home plate, when they introduced her and wheeled her out to join us. She was in a wheelchair because about three months earlier she fell and broke her hip. I was afraid that would prevent her from coming, but she made that long plane trip all the way to New York from Berkeley. She had never seen Yankee Stadium before and I was so proud of her being there.

She was wearing her Yankee cap and a Yankee pinstriped dress that she had made especially for the occasion. They wheeled her to my side, and as I bent over to give her a kiss, she just looked up at me and said, "I look pretty good for an old broad, don't I, Billy?"

I thought she looked beautiful.

She's a tough old bird, my mom. She's eighty-six and she's still so full of life it's unbelievable. Her language tends to get a little salty every once in a while, especially when she talks on her CB. If you're ever in the San Francisco–Oakland area and you have a CB and you make contact with another CBer called "Yankee One," that's my mom.

But now she was here to be part of the festivities while they retired my number. My two half sisters, Joan and Patsy, were there, and my two half brothers, Jack and Frank. My daughter Kelly Ann was there with my two granddaughters, Evie and Sonya. And my son Billy Joe was there. He's a student at Texas Tech University and I'm proud of him because I never had the opportunity to go to college. In fact, Billy Joe is the first member of my family to attend college.

I have been on the field at Yankee Stadium thousands of times, but standing there at home plate on this day was different. Suddenly, the Stadium seemed so much bigger than it ever had before. The stands were almost full and it's an eerie feeling to hear the echo from the loudspeaker, the words just seeming to bounce back at you from the stands.

Bill White, the former great St. Louis Cardinal first baseman and for years a broadcaster for the Yankees, conducted the ceremonies, and I listened intently as he read what had been engraved on my plaque, the words reverberating throughout the huge Stadium.

ALFRED MANUEL "BILLY" MARTIN
CASEY'S BOY

A YANKEE FOREVER. A MAN WHO KNEW ONLY ONE WAY TO PLAY—TO WIN. AS A PLAYER FOR CASEY STENGEL, HE THRIVED ON PRESSURE, DELIVERING THE KEY PLAY OR HIT. MVP OF THE 1953 WORLD SERIES, SETTING RECORD FOR MOST HITS IN SIX-GAME SERIES WITH 12. LATER AS A MANAGER HE BECAME ONE OF THE GREATEST YANKEE MANAGERS.

ERECTED BY
NEW YORK YANKEES
AUGUST 10, 1986

There were telegrams from Joe DiMaggio and Bobby Richardson among others. Ron Luciano, the former American League umpire, made a funny presentation. Brad Corbett, the owner in Texas when I was there (and one of those who fired me), was there with a gift. My buddies Mickey Mantle and Whitey Ford spoke. Ron Guidry presented me with a beautiful No. 1 diamond-and-gold pendant on behalf of the Yankees I had managed.

It was George Steinbrenner who made this day possible. He promised me three years earlier that he was going to give me this day. I never mentioned it to him and I thought he had forgotten about it, but he kept his word and, for that, I'm grateful.

Many of my friends and family, my former

teammates, players and coaches and opponents came from all over the country to be there on my day.

But what really made this day possible was the fans, and to describe what I felt coming down from the stands would be impossible.

As I stood there, waiting for the ceremonies to end, my knees felt like Jell-O. I am an emotional man and this was almost too much to bear. I kept thinking that only twelve other Yankees had had their numbers retired, and how privileged I felt to be joining them. Babe Ruth, No. 3. Lou Gehrig, No. 4. Joe DiMaggio, No. 5. Mickey Mantle, No. 7. Bill Dickey and Yogi Berra, No. 8. Roger Maris, No. 9. Phil Rizzuto, No. 10. Thurman Munson, No. 15. Whitey Ford, No. 16. Elston Howard, No. 32. And, of course, the man who means the most to me, Casey Stengel, No. 37. And now a little dago kid from Berkeley, who was considered too small and not talented enough to make it.

It was my turn to speak and I just didn't know how I was going to get through my speech without breaking down. I didn't.

"The four most important things in my life," I said, "have been my family, God, my friends and being a Yankee. I want to thank all the coaches who helped me in the past; the players who made it possible; and you fans, who are the best in the world, who stuck behind me. I may not have been the greatest Yankee who ever put on the uniform, but I am the proudest."

And that's just about as far as I could get. I wanted to say, "Thank you, Casey Stengel," but I couldn't get it out.

I did remember to send flowers to Casey's grave in Glendale, California. With the flowers, I sent a message that said, "I love you and I owe you everything." This was Casey Stengel's day, too. And it was my mom's day.

I had meant to mention Bobby Richardson and I forgot that, too, but I did send him a letter. Bobby succeeded me as the Yankees' second baseman and he also wore uniform No. 1. I wanted Bobby to know that even though they were retiring No. 1 for me, he is as much entitled to wear that number as I am because of all the honors he received and the dignity he brought to that uniform while wearing it. So if you go to a Yankees' Old Timers' Game and you see Richardson wearing the No. 1 on the back of his uniform, you'll understand why.

That night, at the Sheraton Heights Hotel in Hasbrouck Heights, New Jersey, my day continued at a party given in my honor. The big ballroom was over-flowing with my family and friends. This was all the idea of my fiancée, Jill Guiver, and what a tremendous job she did. Jill spent hours and hours making all the arrangements, and she did almost everything herself, with the support of my attorney, Judge Eddie Sapir of New Orleans, and his associate, Paul Tabary.

Jill assembled the guest list, had the invitations printed, contacted people by telephone. She arranged for the food, the music, the flowers, the liquor. There were people there from all over the country, family and friends and colleagues, some people I hadn't seen since grammar school.

Tom Dreesen, the comedian, a good friend and a very funny man, flew all the way from Hawaii to serve as master of ceremonies and he was sensational as always. Tom brought with him a taped message from Tom Selleck and one from the Chairman of the Board himself, Frank Sinatra.

"I'm the only man in your lifetime who has

been in more saloon fights than you," Frank said. "Billy, you know I love you and have for many, many years."

Ken Kaiser, the American League umpire, spoke, and what touched me was that he had asked the league to switch his assignment from Texas to New York for that day so he could be there. An umpire! Can you believe it?

Jimmy Piersall was there and he said a few words. I once had a knock-down-drag-out fight under the stands with Jimmy when we were both players. Today he is a good friend. A few years ago when Piersall needed a job, I hired him in Texas to do public relations work. Now he was saying, in front of a ballroom filled with people, "If you ever need me, Billy, just call and I'll be there."

Mickey Mantle and Whitey Ford spoke again.

Diane Munson, Thurman's wife, was there with her three children. My old coaches Arthur Fowler and Clete Boyer came, Art from South Carolina, Clete from Atlanta. Mickey Morabito, who helped me so much as public relations director for both the Yankees and the A's, came in from Oakland. Lee MacPhail, the former president of the American League, was there. So were Lou Piniella and several of his players: Ron Guidry, Joe Niekro, Brian Fisher, Dave Righetti and Tommy John.

Jackie Moore, who coached for me in Oakland, was there. So were my old Yankee teammates Joe Collins and Charlie Silvera. And Walt Dropo, who was my teammate in Cincinnati in 1960.

Once again, it was my turn to talk. I wasn't as nervous this time, although I talked without a prepared speech or notes.

"No question, this is the greatest day of my life," I told the people, and I meant it.

"What is Billy Martin?" I asked. "It's you. You are what it's all about, my friends, my family. People came here from all over the United States. That makes me proud.

"I came from Berkeley and people said I was too small to play in the big leagues. They said I couldn't adjust to the big city. I've been up and down and what it boils down to is that the good Lord has taken care of me.

"How do you say thanks? There's no real way. If you have a child that wants to be a major leaguer, God can't give you any more than that. God bless you. I really love you all."

Earlier in the day, at a press conference after the ceremonies at Yankee Stadium, one of the writers asked me what I thought was the reason for my appeal with the fans. I told the writers I thought the people relate to me because I'm a piece of every one of them. I have always managed aggressively and they like that. And they like the fact that I have told my bosses what they can do with their jobs; I have stood up to my bosses. And I think every working man would like to do that. He would like to stand up to his boss, to tell his boss to take this job and stick it. I always fought for what I thought was right and that's why the average guy relates to me.

To prove the point, one of the nicest things that happened to me that night, at the party, was that the members of the New York City Police Department detail that works Yankee Stadium presented me with a gift. They know of my interest in the Civil War and they gave me an original photograph of General Sheridan. That thrilled me because these are just hardworking guys, certainly not millionaires, and they were kind enough and considerate enough to do something for me. I don't know how to thank them. To me, these guys represent the average fans, who have always been my biggest supporters.

The writers also asked me about the possibility of managing the Yankees again. I told them I'm not coming back again as manager of the Yankees. Look, I don't know what's going to happen. I can't read the future. I do know that I meant it when I said it at the time. And I think the reason I felt that way is this: To wear that uniform was an awfully proud thing. To think of the people who wore it—Babe Ruth, Lou Gehrig, Joe DiMaggio—and to have your plaque up there with theirs, well, that's something special. They talk about the Pride of the Yankees. I know about it because it has always been in me. Even when I was with other teams, I still considered myself a Yankee.

Then, when I was brought back as manager of the Yankees, that just topped everything off. It was my dream come true. I wanted to manage the Yankees so badly; I loved that job so much. And as with anything that you love so much, it hurts even more when you lose it. Maybe I said I'd never manage the Yankees again because I don't want to go through the pain of losing that job again.

Tom Lasorda says that when he dies and goes to heaven, he'll find the Lord wearing Dodger blue. Tom Lasorda is wrong. When he dies and goes to heaven, he'll find the Lord wearing Yankee pinstripes.

2

It was only an exhibition game, so I figured this was as good a time as any to try out a new play I had thought about and worked on that spring. I was managing the Detroit Tigers at the time and we were playing against the Texas Rangers, managed by Ted Williams.

Some people say Ted Williams was the greatest hitter of all time. I wouldn't dispute that, although I never saw Ty Cobb, Honus Wagner, Rogers Hornsby or Babe Ruth. Let's just say that Williams certainly was *one* of the greatest hitters of all time. Also one of the lousiest managers of all time.

As a rule, great players don't make good managers. The reason is that superstars seem to lack the patience to accept mediocrity in their players and, let's face it, the majority of your players are going to be average or mediocre. Having been blessed with such natural talent, superstars never had to struggle to be successful players. Things came so easy to them, they didn't have to work as hard as a journeyman did. And they couldn't seem to understand why most of their players could not do the things they could do.

A guy like me, who had to battle and scrap and fight for everything, usually has a better chance of making it as a manager. We have had to look at every angle in order to survive as players. We tried to get every edge. And that's going to be an asset to you when you manage.

Ted Williams proves the point about superstars as managers. Great hitter. Great hitting instructor. Lousy manager. In four seasons, his teams never finished higher than fourth. Only once did he have a winning percentage over .500. And his total record as a manager was 273–364.

Anyway, on this particular day we were playing the Texas Rangers an exhibition game and it was time for me to try out this trick play. We had runners on first and third with two outs. All of a sudden, my runner on first breaks for second. Now Williams thinks he has an easy out, which is exactly what I wanted him to think.

"Pick that son of a bitch off," he shouts from their bench.

So the Texas pitcher throws over to first to pick my runner off. But the runner delays the pickoff by purposely getting himself caught in a rundown between first and second. As soon as the pitcher throws over to first, the runner on third breaks for home. And while the Texas infielders are occupied with the runner on first, my guy scores from third. Even though it's the third out at first, the run counts if the runner crosses home plate before the out is made. It works every time.

Williams is watching all this and he shakes his head, looks at me and shouts, "Well, I learned something."

"Yeah," I said. "Thank you very much."

One basic rule for any manager is to manage according to his personnel. A good manager doesn't try to adapt his personnel to his style of managing; a good manager changes his style of managing to suit his personnel. Of course, you always try to get your front office to acquire the kind of players that fit best into your style of managing. But sometimes those players are not immediately available. It might take a while to get them, and until you do, you might have to adjust your style of managing to the team you have.

This does not contradict the fact that sometimes—not very often—you may have to ask a player to do something that is not suited to his physical skills. For example, you may have your slowest runner steal, or you may bunt with a guy who is not a very good bunter. What you're counting on there is the element of surprise. Sometimes you might try to force things, like take an extra base, just to try to get the other team to make a mistake. But, as I say, that's the exception, not the rule, and you don't want to do that too often for fear of losing the element of surprise.

In Minnesota, I had a couple of guys who could run and steal a base (Cesar Tovar had 45 stolen bases, Rod Carew had 19), but I also had guys who could hit the ball out of the ballpark (Harmon Killebrew led the major leagues with 49 homers, Tony Oliva had 24). So I used both weapons. I wasn't going to run in a situation when I would lose Killebrew's bat, either by having a runner thrown out for the last out of an inning or by leaving a base open so the other team could walk Harmon, my most dangerous and productive hitter.

On offense, I basically managed around Killebrew's bat—always trying to get him to the plate with runners on base, always trying to make certain the other team couldn't pitch around him. I didn't want Harmon leading off an inning if I could help it. That's why I would put the reins on my base stealers if Killebrew was coming to bat.

Oliva led the league with 197 hits when we won the division championship in Minnesota in 1969. He also drew 45 walks, so he was the perfect hitter to bat in front of Killebrew, my cleanup man. That meant that more than two hundred times when Harmon came to bat, Oliva was on base, so there were plenty of opportunities for Killebrew to drive in runs. And he did. That year Harmon led the majors with 140 RBIs.

To protect Killebrew and make certain that he would get pitches to hit or that he wouldn't be walked too often, I batted Rich Reese behind him. Reese was a big, strong left-handed line drive and contact hitter and he had a good year for me, with 16 homers and 69 RBIs and a .322 batting average. He helped Killebrew have his big year by being a threat to hit the long ball. As it was, Harmon still led the league with 145 walks.

Once Killebrew was disposed of, and my big bat was gone, that's when I'd use the other weapons I had at my command—the steal, hit-and-run. Carew stole home seven times in 1969, my one season as manager of the Twins. Pete Reiser of the Brooklyn Dodgers set the major league record for stealing home in 1946, when he stole seven times. Carew tied it in 1969 and their record still stands. Carew should have had the record to himself. The next time he tried to steal home he knocked the umpire on his rear as he came across

home plate. The ump called him out, but to this day I
believe that was the eighth time Carew stole home in
1969.

When I won a division title with Detroit in
1972, we had an older team, guys who could hit home
runs like Norm Cash, Bill Freehan, Al Kaline, Willie
Horton and Jim Northrup. We hit 122 home runs that
year and stole only 17 bases (the Indians were second
from the bottom in steals and they had 49). So it was
obvious we had to play for the big inning and win with
power, defense and pitching.

Texas was like Minnesota. Jeff Burroughs was
my Harmon Killebrew with the Rangers. He hit 25
home runs and led the league with 118 RBIs and was
the Most Valuable Player in the American League. So I
managed around Jeff's at bats like I did with Harmon
Killebrew in Minnesota, and I had Davey Nelson,
Lenny Randle and Cesar Tovar who could steal a base.

When I came to New York I had a team that
had only Mickey Rivers and Willie Randolph who could
run. In 1975, the year before he came to the Yankees,
Rivers led the American League in stolen bases with 70.
He could easily have been a 100-stolen-base man if the
situation dictated it. It just wasn't necessary for him to
run that much with the Yankees because we had left-
handed power with Reggie Jackson, Chris Chambliss
and Graig Nettles. As a result, I kept the wraps on
Rivers and Randolph. Mickey stole 43 bases in 1976 and
22 in 1977. Willie stole 37 and 13. But I didn't need
them to steal a lot of bases. Instead, I played for the big
inning, looking for the long ball, especially in Yankee
Stadium, where you must have left-handed pitching
and left-handed power hitting to be successful.

Oakland? A completely different story. We
were always among the leaders in stolen bases, mainly

because of Rickey Henderson. He became my offensive leader and I managed around him. If Rickey got on base, we produced runs. It was as simple as that. I let Rickey run. Every chance he got, he was stealing. I had one of the game's greatest base stealers of all time, so I took advantage of his skill. Only a fool wouldn't.

I didn't make Henderson into a great base stealer. The skill was always there. All I did was encourage him to use the gifts God gave him and capitalize on his natural ability. The year before I arrived, he had stolen only 33 bases, which I thought was a waste of his talent. So I made him run more often and, in 1980, my first year in Oakland, he stole 100 bases, the first player in American League history to steal that many. In 1982, my last year in Oakland, Rickey stole 130 bases, an all-time record.

If you have a guy who can't bunt, you don't ask him to bunt. It may be a bunt situation, but your hitter is not a good bunter, so you don't bunt. Why ask a man to do something he can't do? All you're doing is giving up an out, plus that hitter's bat.

There are exceptions. You might do it for the element of surprise. If Dave Winfield is at bat, the other team is not looking for him to bunt. Dave is not a bad bunter, it's just that it's not often that he's asked to bunt. So with Winfield batting, you have the element of surprise going for you. The third baseman is back. He's not expecting a bunt. You know if Winfield lays one down, he's got a base hit. So you might ask him to bunt for the hit, to put another man on base and move the runners along. It could lead to a big run or a big inning that can win you a game.

I won a playoff game once by using the element of surprise. One play can turn a game around and one game can turn a series and a season around and that's what happened in the fifth game of the 1977 playoffs against Kansas City.

It was a situation in which the bunt was in order. The book called for it. Everybody expected it. Instead, I had my hitter hit away to cross up the defense and it worked. I went against the book and it paid off and that one play turned the playoffs around.

We had been trailing throughout the game after the Royals scored two in the first inning off Ron Guidry in the deciding game of the playoffs. We scored a run in the third to make it 2–1 and the Royals came back with a run in the bottom of the third to make it 3–1. We got another run in the eighth to make it 3–2 and that's how it stood going into the ninth inning. We were down to our last three outs of the season and we were playing on the road.

Paul Blair opened the ninth with a single. Then I sent Roy White up as a pinch hitter and he drew a walk. Now we had runners on first and second, none out and the top of our batting order coming up, Mickey Rivers followed by Willie Randolph, Thurman Munson and Lou Piniella.

Royals manager Whitey Herzog brought in a left-hander, Larry Gura, to face Rivers and everybody in the ballpark figured Mickey was going to lay down a bunt to move the tying run to third and the lead run to second. That was the "book" play. The Royals figured Rivers was going to bunt and I figured that was what they figured. But I had other ideas.

The first baseman and third baseman were playing in, looking for the bunt. And they would be moving with the pitch. Second baseman Frank White was also moving, cheating toward first, getting ready to cover the bag after the bunt. With all that happening, I figured Rivers' chances of driving the ball through the infield were improved maybe 50 percent. Besides, even if he didn't get the ball through, with Mickey's speed and the infield moving, it was unlikely they were going to get a double play. I figured it was worth the gamble to go against the book and try to blow the game open with a big inning.

I gave Rivers the hit sign and he drove a shot through the right side, only a few feet from where White was playing. If White had not been cheating toward first, it probably would have been a double play. Instead, Blair scored from second to tie the game and Roy White went to third with the winning run. We didn't break the game open, but we scored three runs and took a 5–3 lead and Sparky Lyle held them in the bottom of the ninth. We won the American League pennant and went on to beat the Los Angeles Dodgers in the World Series, all because I refused to go by the book.

I had taken a gamble. Sure, it was the ideal bunt situation. Sure, the book called for the bunt. Sure, I went against the book. And if Mickey had hit into a double play, I would have been criticized from here to Cooperstown. George Steinbrenner would have been on my back so fast you would have thought he was Hulk Hogan. But I figured it was worth the gamble. A calculated gamble, to be sure, but a gamble nonetheless. As I say, a good manager has to have the courage of his convictions. He has to have the guts to be willing to take a chance once in a while. As a manager, I think I have had the courage of my convictions and the guts to take a chance. How many managers, for instance, have three different bunt signs?

I do. I have one sign for a sacrifice bunt, one for a squeeze bunt and a third when I want the hitter to bunt for a base hit.

When the batter drops a bunt and the runner on first goes to third base, it's not just by accident that it happens. He was ordered to do it. It's something I worked on and developed and have used a lot, especially in Oakland.

If I give the hitter a sign to bunt for a base hit, that means he has to lay down a bunt; he has no choice. Because, at the same time, I have also given the runner on first base the steal sign.

When I had Rickey Henderson and Dwayne Murphy in Oakland, I would use this play a lot with Rickey on first and Murph batting. I'd give Murphy the sign to bunt for a base hit. At the same time, I'd give Henderson the steal sign. Now, Murphy bunts toward third, and with Rickey running on the pitch, he can go all the way to third base with his speed because the catcher usually forgets to cover third. Now I have runners on first and third. Even if Murphy is thrown out at first, which rarely happened, I still have a runner on third and he can score on a fly ball to the outfield or even an infield out.

I taught that play all spring training when I first took over the Oakland club, but we didn't get a chance to execute it for about the first two weeks of the season. The situation just never arose in those first two weeks. Finally, when the situation did arise, I put on the play and it worked to perfection. A cheer went up from our bench, you would have thought we'd just won the pennant.

As a manager, I like to stay on top of things. I want control over everything on the field. From the bench I will give my pitcher a sign to pick the runner off first or I will give a sign for the pitchout or a sign for the catcher to pick the runner off first.

I wrote the form for the Yankees' scouting reports. I told them what I wanted to know, not what they wanted to tell me. The little things I want to know to get an edge. Will the other manager squeeze? Does he like to hit-and-run a lot? On what count? With which players? Who's swinging the bat well for them? I like my scouts to scout the other managers as well as the players.

There is very little that is new in the game of baseball. It's still basically the same game that Abner Doubleday invented, if he really did invent it. For more than a hundred years, the fundamentals of the game have hardly changed at all. Unlike other sports, the rules are just about the same as they always were, and the layout of the field and the deployment of the players on defense haven't changed.

The bases are still ninety feet apart, the pitcher is still sixty feet, six inches, from the batter. It's remarkable when you think of it.

It's for this reason, I believe, that the role of the manager is more important in baseball than that of the coach in football, basketball or hockey. There's very little that's new in baseball except what a sharp, alert manager can think of to get an edge. There isn't a great deal of opportunity for innovation in baseball, but every little bit helps and I have been as innovative as anyone during my managerial career.

I have already told you about my three bunt signs and the play I devised in which, with runners on first and third, the runner on first purposely gets himself picked off and caught in a rundown so the runner on third can score.

Here's another play I thought of. Let's say we're playing the Kansas City Royals and Willie Wilson gets on first. Wilson is a great base stealer and he's always looking for the opportunity to steal second. I

might have my first baseman, Don Mattingly, play behind the runner, instead of holding him on. Instinctively, Wilson thinks Mattingly is ignoring him, or has
made a mistake. Now he thinks he's going to steal second base easily. So he takes off for second on the first
pitch. And, of course, that's exactly what I want him to
do because I have called for a pitchout. In other words,
we have lulled the runner into a false sense of security
by pretending to ignore him. And I'm anticipating that
he's going to think he's being ignored and he's going to
try to steal second. And what happens? We're ready for
him and we throw him out easily.

I also devised a play that is being used quite a
bit now. It's a defensive play against the bunt. I'm the
guy who started the play where the third baseman
charges the bunt and the shortstop, instead of covering
second base, dashes for third. You'd be surprised how
often we get the runner going from second to third.

And of course, no manager has made better or
more successful use of the squeeze play or the steal of
home than I have.

Baseball is constantly changing. Not major
changes, but subtle ones, and you have to be ready for
those changes. For every offensive adjustment, there
has to be a defensive countermove, and for every defensive adjustment, there has to be an offensive countermove. And, again, the fact that things have been
done the same way for a hundred years doesn't make
them right.

As long as I have been around this game, I
have heard baseball people say that you have to protect
the foul lines with your first baseman and third baseman late in the game when the score is close. Why?
Because that's the way it's been done for a hundred
years.

The theory is that you don't want to give the hitter an extra base. You don't want to allow the tying or winning run to get to second. You will concede them first base, but not second.

I don't concede anything. If you want to save a base, save first base. Cut off the single and don't worry about the double. Play the percentages. More balls are hit in the holes between first and second and between second and third than are hit down the lines.

The Kansas City Royals won the sixth game of the 1985 World Series because the St. Louis Cardinals were protecting the line against Steve Balboni. So Balboni got a hit on a ball that the third baseman might have handled under ordinary conditions. Instead of an out, or even a double play, the Royals had runners on first and second and none out. And both runners came around to score and the Cardinals lost, 2–1, because they protected the line.

I tell my coaches I don't want the third baseman and first baseman hugging the lines in that situation. I want them where they can reach the line, but I am more interested in knocking off the single in the hole.

In recent years, we have seen the increasing use of computers in baseball. Computers are used for scouting purposes, for making out lineups, for determining what hitters hit which pitchers best. I have nothing against progress and modern technology. I have nothing against computers in general. I have even used them to keep stats on hitters vs. pitchers, pitchers vs. hitters, who's doing what with men on base, who's hitting in the late innings. The problem with computers, I think, is that they are only as good as the brain that programs them and feeds them. If you have a dummy putting the data in the computer, what good is the computer?

There are some things a computer can't tell you. It can't tell you the situation in the game when an individual got a hit off a certain pitcher. It doesn't tell you the score, the inning, the count. It doesn't measure aggressiveness, hustle and the heart of the player. All it tells you is plain, cold statistics, and statistics don't tell the whole story. I'd much rather trust my eyes or the eyes of one of my scouts.

I learned about how meaningless statistics are thirty-five years ago when the Yankees were competing with the Red Sox for the American League pennant almost every year.

In 1950, the Red Sox had seven .300 hitters, the batting champ and the RBI champs. In 1951, they had three .300 hitters, we had one and we had no batter with more than 88 RBIs. The year before I got there, 1949, the Yankees had one .300 hitter and their leading RBI man was Yogi Berra with 91. The Red Sox had four .300 hitters and three guys with more than 100 RBIs, including Ted Williams and Vern Stephens, who tied for the league lead with 159. But the Yankees won the pennant all three years and the Red Sox finished either second or third. So what does that tell you about statistics? That they're not worth a damn, that's what.

3

In my major league career, I played for ten different managers and, without question, Casey Stengel stood head and shoulders above them all. I have played for some good managers and some bad ones, but I always tried to take something from each of them. Even the bad ones. Maybe what I took from the bad ones was how not to do something, but I learned from each of my managers.

Next to Stengel, Charlie Dressen was the best manager I played for. Dressen had replaced Stengel in Oakland after Casey went to New York in 1949. Charlie had managed Cincinnati without much success from 1934 through 1937, and he coached for the Yankees and Dodgers before coming to Oakland. Later, he would win pennants for the Brooklyn Dodgers in 1952 and 1953, and of course my Yankees beat him in the World Series both times. In 1952 I made that catch of a wind-blown pop fly on a ball hit by Jackie Robinson with two outs and the bases loaded. And in 1953 I set the World Series record for hits.

After the 1953 season, Charlie's wife wrote a letter to Walter O'Malley, the owner of the Dodgers, demanding a two-year contract. The Dodgers didn't believe in giving their managers two-year contracts and Mr. O'Malley obviously was teed off at the letter. He fired Dressen and replaced him with an unknown minor league manager named Walter Alston.

Later, Dressen managed the Washington Senators from 1955 through early 1957 and the Milwaukee Braves in 1960 and 1961. He finished his managerial career with the Detroit Tigers from 1963 through early 1966.

I really liked that man. He was hard to get to know, but after you got to know him, you realized he was a softie at heart.

Charlie was a little guy and he had this tough way of talking. He had played professional football with the old Decatur Staleys, which was a team in the early days of pro football, long before television. The Staleys were owned by George Halas and actually were the ancestors of the Chicago Bears.

You had to be tough to make it as a pro football player in those days and Charlie was tough, especially for a guy who stood about five-foot-five and weighed maybe 150 tops. In fact, Dressen was a much better football player than he was a baseball player. But in those days—I'm talking about the 1920s—pro football was not on a par with baseball in popularity or in the amount of money that could be made in the game.

Charlie played baseball for eight years in the major leagues, as an infielder with the Cincinnati Reds and New York Giants. In eight seasons, he hit a total of 11 home runs and had a lifetime batting average of .272, which would be considered good today but was weak in those days.

One of Charlie's teammates when he played in Cincinnati was Leo Durocher. The two became good friends and it was easy to understand why. They were like two peas in a pod, both little, both tough, both egotistical and both brilliant strategists. After Dressen got fired as manager of the Reds, Durocher took him on as a coach with the Dodgers. And, of course, Dressen eventually managed the Dodgers himself.

When I first met Charlie, I didn't like him at all. He had a tendency to brag a lot. He had a tremendous ego and it was always "I did this" and "I did that," never "we" or "they" or "the team." That pissed off a lot of people, especially his players, and I admit it pissed me off, too, at first. Then I realized that it was just the way he was and I began to accept it. Later, I found out what a nice man Charlie really was. He loved to cook and he was always cooking something up in the ballpark. His favorites were crab claws and chili and he would cook up batches and invite the players to come in and feast.

As a baseball strategist, there was none better than Dressen. He was brilliant. I learned so much from him—when to hit-and-run, on what count to steal, how to pitch hitters, how to steal signs. Dressen was the best I ever saw at stealing signs. In fact, there's a story that when he managed the All-Star team one year, he called the players together for a meeting before the game. Somebody asked about signals.

"Just use the ones you use during the regular

season with your own teams," Charlie said. "I know them all."

Freddy Hutchinson was another manager I liked and enjoyed playing for. I was with him only one year in Cincinnati, but I really came to respect him. To look at him, you would think he was the meanest man in America. Central Casting would have no trouble placing him as Scrooge. He rarely smiled and he had this hangdog expression. But, in this case at least, looks were deceiving. Freddy Hutchinson was one of the warmest, nicest and gentlest men I ever knew.

He was a chain-smoker and it cost him his life. He died of throat cancer in 1964. The irony of that is that his brother was one of the foremost cancer surgeons in the country, out of Seattle, Washington.

Freddy had an excellent career as a pitcher with the Detroit Tigers in the 1940s and 1950s. He never won 20, but one year he was 18–10 and another year he was 17–8.

He wasn't a great manager, but Hutchinson did win a pennant with the Reds in 1961, which was the year after I was there (no connection). He knew how to deal with people and he naturally knew how to handle pitchers. From him, I learned a lot about handling pitchers—when a pitcher is tired and should come out, to have patience with certain pitchers, to get pitchers to give you a little bit more when they think they don't have any more to give.

It's funny, though. For some reason—and I'm speaking generally—pitchers don't make good managers. You would think they would because they have to be in the game all the time, they have to know hitters' weaknesses and they certainly know about pitching, which is the most important aspect of the game. But they don't.

The only former pitcher who has been successful as a manager in the twenty years since I have been
managing is Tommy Lasorda. Of course, he never was a
very good major league pitcher. In fact, he never even
won a game in the big leagues as a pitcher. He was a
struggler all his life and that's probably why he's a good
manager. As I said before, the guys who had to struggle
as players, the so-called journeymen, make the best
managers. Superstars do not.

There are exceptions to everything, but generally speaking, middle infielders make the best managers. Second basemen and shortstops and, to a lesser
degree, third basemen. John McGraw, Joe Cronin,
Durocher, Bucky Harris, Frankie Frisch, Hughie Jen-
nings, Miller Huggins. All infielders.

Catchers are good. Connie Mack was a
catcher. So were Al Lopez, Gabby Street and Wilbert
Robinson. And Branch Rickey also was a catcher.

Again, it's an exception to the rule, but the
worst manager I ever played for was Joe Gordon. And
he was a second baseman and a great one. I had him as
my manager for one year in Cleveland.

I liked Joe as a person. But as a manager he was
a disaster. He never thought ahead and was always
getting outmaneuvered. He didn't prepare for what
might happen two innings later. His biggest problem
was that he played favorites. If he didn't like you, that
was it; you'd had it with him. And he wouldn't play you
even if you were better than the guy playing ahead of
you. He formed these likes and dislikes for players and
it clouded his judgment. A manager can't do that.

One year I played winter ball for Gordon in
Modesto and somebody said I was a better second baseman than he was. Well, that was all Joe had to hear. The
next day, he benched me. That's what I mean about

Gordon letting little things color his judgment as a manager. Still, I learned from him. I learned what not to do. I saw things he did and I tried to avoid doing those same things.

Now I'm probably going to get myself in trouble. I'm going to rate some of my contemporaries as managers. As I say, this will probably get me in trouble, but what the hell, I'm used to that. I can't help it. I have to say what I feel and what I think. I have always done that.

Before I rate the current managers, though, a word about my successor, Lou Piniella. First, let me admit that I was doubtful that Lou would make a good manager. Oh, he knows the game and he knows how to deal with people. I knew that. My doubts were based purely on the fact that Lou had never managed anywhere. He wasn't even a coach on the lines. And I feel very strongly that you need to experience what it is like to manage before you can be successful as a manager.

But as a rookie manager, Piniella did a good job considering the weakness of his pitching staff, largely due to injury. He handled the pitchers better than I thought he would. I like the way he does things. He handled the job with class and the press loves him. Believe me, I pulled for Lou all year. I offered him my advice if he wanted to take it. I told him I would be available whenever he wanted to talk. And we did get together several times during the season, on the road.

Let me also say that of the players still playing, the one I think will make the best manager—if he wants to manage—is Graig Nettles. He's sharp and a competitor. And he started out as a second baseman.

To me, the best manager available is a guy who has never managed in the major leagues, my old third base coach at Oakland, Clete Boyer. If I was the general manager of a team, I'd hire Clete to manage my team in a minute. Now, my evaluation of the current managers.

Let me emphasize that what I have to say about these managers has nothing to do with what I think about them as men. I'm talking about their managerial ability—from the point of view of someone who has had to manage against them. Just as the best way to judge a pitcher is to hit against him and the best way to judge a gin rummy player is to play against him, the best way to rate a manager is to manage against him.

Tommy Lasorda: I haven't managed against him very often, except in the World Series of 1977. I enjoy kidding with him. In the 1977 World Series, we won the first game in Yankee Stadium and they won the second game. Before the third game, in Los Angeles, when we met at home plate with the umpires, I told him, "Your ass has had it, buddy. You better enjoy that victory because we're going to kick your ass."

And we did. Beat them in six games.

Tommy's strength as a manager seems to be as a motivator, a positive thinker. But all that hugging and everything with his players, I don't believe in it. Graig Nettles had the best comment about that.

"Hey, Skip," he said. "If we ever get those guys broken up, we're gonna beat them."

To me, Tommy Lasorda is a professional bull-shitter. I don't say that derogatorily. And I don't resent it. I think that's his true nature. He likes to do things like that, to tell stories and jokes. He's great for the game of baseball, kind of a latter-day Casey Stengel. He really enjoys being funny. He's trying to be a comedian and a manager at the same time and he gets a big kick out of doing it. Besides, it works for him. He's been very successful as a manager, one of the few pitchers who have. I couldn't be that way. Tommy's different. That's his thing and if it works, and he's not a phony about it, more power to him.

Dick Williams: A very good manager. Tough on players, a disciplinarian, but he's been very successful. Also a journeyman player. I believe a guy manages the way he played. Yogi Berra was easygoing as a player and he was easygoing as a manager. Dick Williams was very aggressive as a player, and he's very aggressive as a manager. He's also won pennants with three teams. I like his style.

Gene Mauch: To me, he's the classic case of the guy who overmanages. He tries to be so brilliant. He takes the game away from his players. His problem is that he often tries to show how much he knows, how much more he knows about the game than the guy in the other dugout, and it often backfires on him. He takes himself out of more games than any manager I ever managed against. The game is not as complicated as he makes it. I think he tries to make it more complex than it really is.

I love managing against Mauch. Usually, I'm a very aggressive manager, but against Mauch I turn conservative. I let him make his moves and I just sit back and wait until he outsmarts himself. I've caught him using up his players too early, so that he's left with no extra men in the late innings. I'll sit back, say, until he's used up all his right-handed hitters, then I'll bring in my left-handed relief pitcher. Gene is also big on the bunt. He likes to play for one run, which means he's giving up outs early in the game. This is one of those cases where I often manage against the other manager instead of against the other team.

Don't get me wrong, Gene is a brilliant baseball man and it's a challenge to go up against him, to try to outthink and outguess him. But I like managing against him because I feel that sooner or later he's going to outsmart himself. He's the Little General, but after I beat him I won't say anything. He'll make all these moves and they'll be brilliant and I'll just make him think he's so intelligent. He can take the bows for his moves. I'll take the victory.

Bobby Cox: He gave up managing to become a general manager in Atlanta and that surprised me because he was right at the height of his success. I liked the way he managed. He managed just enough. He didn't overmanage. He's brilliant. He worked hard to get where he did, managing several years in the minor leagues, working his way up to a coach before getting his shot as a manager. He deserves every bit of his success.

After his Toronto Blue Jays beat us out for the American League East title in 1985, I wanted to see him do well in the playoffs. But I had a dilemma. It was tough for me to root in the League Championship Series because the guy Bobby was managing against was Dick Howser, another one of my guys. They were both my coaches in New York and I like them both, so I was torn between which one I wanted to see win.

Dick Howser: An outstanding manager. He's exceptional in every phase of the game and the success he's had reflects that. He knows how to teach, he knows how to handle his players and he handles the press and his front office a hell of a lot better than I do. He's got great rapport with people, period. He knows how to talk to people. I don't. For some reason, I can go into a restaurant where I'm not known, walk up to the maître d' and ask for a table for two.

"JUST A MINUTE," the maître d' will shout.

Howser can go up to the same maître d' and ask for a table for two in the same way, and guess what?

"Yes, sir, Mr. Howser, I'll be right with you."

So you know what I do? I'll tell the person I'm with to go to the maître d' and ask for the table, because I know if I do it, I might not get the proper service or the proper table, or I'm going to get into an argument with the guy. Do you think I'm paranoid about this? Well, I guess I am a little, but it's happened so many times.

I have digressed from my original point, which is that Dick Howser is an outstanding manager. But part of his success comes from the way he deals with people.

In addition to being a great manager, Dick is also a great friend and he was a loyal coach for me. That's why I was so heartbroken when I heard about his illness. Right after the 1986 All-Star Game, doctors discovered that Dick had a tumor on his brain. It was affecting his personality and his managing. He first complained about headaches and a pain in his neck. But his third base coach, Mike Ferraro, another of my former coaches, noticed that Dick was forgetting names and dates and he told the team trainer, who told the team doctor. They found that the tumor was malignant and they operated, but they could only remove part of it. When I heard that, I was sick. I immediately went to church and lit a candle for Dick and his wife, Nancy, and I sent them a telegram telling them that I knew Dick would beat this thing because he's always been a fighter.

John McNamara: I like Johnny Mac as a friend. As a manager, his style is very different from mine. John is a lot like Bob Lemon: just put the team out there and let them go at it. That's not my style of managing. I disagree with John as a manager on some points, just as I disagree with Lemon on some points. Not that they're not good baseball men; they are. But their style is to undermanage, to be laid-back. They're too laid-back for my tastes.

That doesn't mean I'm right and they're wrong. They both have been successful, so they must be doing something right. It's just that I don't think their style would work for me. Johnny Mac and Lem are both such nice guys and I feel if you're too nice a guy, the players will shit on you. And, in the end, it's your ass, not theirs. John is such a good guy, he let sentiment get the better of him in the 1986 World Series. Normally he would have removed Bill Buckner with a lead in the bottom of the ninth inning, but in the sixth game he didn't and it cost him.

Pat Corrales: A good manager who keeps improving. Sometimes he has a tendency to overmanage, but he's a good person and a very aggressive manager. He also has a temper. He's been on the field a few times in the middle of fights. I keep telling him, "Hey, Pat, you have to learn to control your temper."

Bobby Valentine: He's new and inexperienced and it's hard for me to rate him because I managed against him only at the tail end of the 1985 season. It seemed to me that he had a lot to learn then. I think he suffered from the fact that he never managed in the minor leagues. But judging by the way he improved his team in 1986, he must have learned from his experience. He's bright and he should keep getting better.

George Bamberger: Another of those Lemon–McNamara types. Low-key and easygoing. He won't rock the boat and he won't dazzle you with moves and strategy, but he knows the game. One thing he does know is pitching. He was a successful pitching coach for the Baltimore Orioles when they had that great staff of Jim Palmer, Mike Cuellar, Dave McNally and Pat Dobson. George is great with young pitchers and his team always reflects that. When you play Bambi's team, you know you're not going to score a lot of runs.

Davey Johnson: Because he's in the National League, I didn't get a chance to manage against him. But since we were both managing in New York, I got to see many of his games on television. And I spent some time with him at banquets and at the baseball meetings. From what I could see, I like his style. And from our conversations, I like his philosophy. Also, his record has been outstanding, and he proved just how good a manager he is by going all the way in 1986.

Tony LaRussa: A good manager. He tries to improve himself all the time. Every year he tries something new, something different, which I feel is very important for a manager. You must change constantly and improve or the game will pass you by. I like Tony and it bothered me when those stories came out that the White Sox were talking to me about replacing him. But that's baseball and I'm sure Tony understood that's one of the hazards of the job. Every manager does. Or should. I didn't go to the White Sox people, they came to me. Besides, I was fired myself a few times and I never held it against the guy who took my job.

Sparky Anderson: Overrated. I don't think he's that good a manager. I don't think he knows pitching well enough. Look at what happened once Roger Craig left him as pitching coach. Also, I think players have a tendency to manage Sparky instead of the other way around. You can't do that. You can't have different sets of rules for different players like Sparky does. I know he's been successful and he has a great record. But he's been successful because he's had great teams. And when you have good teams, you're going to be successful as a manager. He had a great team in Cincinnati. And he has a great team in Detroit. But after he ran away with everything in 1984, the Tigers fell right on their asses in 1985 and I think the reason they did is that Sparky didn't know how to stop complacency.

Now, don't jump to conclusions. Sparky Anderson is a very entertaining guy, and you can't take away what he has done as a manager. I especially respect one thing about Sparky: He's 100 percent baseball all the time. He loves the game, like we all do, and he's one of the foremost ambassadors of the game. A lot like Casey was. He's promoting our game and I respect him for that.

Earl Weaver: I saved the best for last. I'm not being facetious when I say that. I know we're supposed to have a hot rivalry going between us. The way that started is that I didn't like him when he first came into the league. Frankly, he pissed me off the way he strutted around like a little bantam rooster and the way he talked. Thought he knew it all. Then he beat me three straight playoff games in 1969 when I was with Minnesota and that got me fired.

Later, when I came back with Detroit, he was always making comments about me in the papers, and I would return them with comments of my own. During the game, I'd be in my dugout and he'd be in his and I'd hear his raspy voice yelling at the umpires or at one of my players. I'd jump up to the top step of the dugout to say something to him, but he'd run away and hide. Even when he didn't run, I wouldn't be able to look him in the eye, anyway, because he's so short.

Sometimes, he wouldn't even be there; he'd be down in the runway, yelling at somebody and lighting up one of the cigarettes that he carries inside his uniform shirt.

Our rivalry is real. It's based on the fact that

we try so hard to beat each other and have gone head to head for a championship so many times. I think we have more a grudging respect for one another than a true rivalry.

As a manager, Earl likes to play for the big inning. He thinks the sacrifice bunt is overrated and he likes to build his teams around pitching, defense and power. His trademark is the three-run homer. He's been the most successful manager of my time, but then he's had the best teams. It's hard to imagine Earl Weaver not managing a major league baseball team in 1987.

I got to know him better at the baseball meetings and I realized this is a hell of a guy. Then I started to really appreciate the way he managed. I love managing against him because of the challenge. As a manager, Earl does it all. He knows how to be aggressive and he knows his players and he knows how to use them. He knows what they can do and what they can't do and he's great at playing to his strengths, which all good managers do.

If I have one criticism about him it's that he overdoes it with umpires. I know that's going to make some people laugh, because I have a reputation for being hard on umpires. Oh, sure, I like to go out there and give them hell, yell and scream and kick some dirt if I think an umpire has blown a call against me. But believe me, I have great rapport with umpires and the reason I do is that I never carry a grudge. If I have an argument with an umpire, no matter how vicious and nasty it gets, I don't carry it over to the next game. It's gone. Finished. I'll talk to that same umpire the next day and we'll bury the hatchet right there. Umpires appreciate that. I know they do because they have told me so.

Most of them will tell you, "Billy will give you a hell of an argument, but he doesn't carry it over the next day and he's fair."

I'm afraid my buddy Earl doesn't do that. He carries it over and I think it hurts him. Good. Let it. I'll take any edge I can get against him. But in every other phase of managing, Earl is outstanding, and his record proves it.

Getting to know him, I found out something else about Weaver that I didn't know. The guy has a sense of humor.

There was a story in the paper a few years ago about how Earl was managing a game against the Minnesota Twins, first base was open and Earl ordered his pitcher to walk the next hitter. Jim Palmer, whose battles with Weaver are legendary, is sitting on the other end of the bench, but when he sees the intentional walk being issued, he comes storming down to Weaver's side of the bench in a rage.

"We're walking Danny Ford to get to Larry Hisle," Palmer is shouting. "I can't believe it. The man's crazy."

"That's not Ford," Earl says in his most irritated voice. "That's Hisle we're walking."

"Well, you better look again," says Palmer.

And sure enough, Earl had been so engrossed in the game he got mixed up. Hisle and Ford are both black, they're both right-handed hitters and they are about the same height and weight. Earl must have looked at the wrong line on his lineup card, because Ford was the batter getting the intentional walk and Hisle, the Twins' best RBI man, was on deck. Ford got the walk and Hisle got up and got a base hit.

The next day I'm in Kansas City in the visiting

manager's office and I put in a call to the visiting manager's office in Minnesota. Weaver answers.

"Earl," I said, "this is Billy. What's up?"

It's not unusual for managers to call one another and just shoot the bull, even during the season. So I talked with him for a few minutes, just making small talk. Finally I said, "Hey, Earl, I know you're trying to beat me out of a pennant and I'm trying to beat you, but can I ask you one question? We're going to Minnesota after we leave here and I just want to ask your advice on something. How do I tell the difference between Danny Ford and Larry Hisle?"

Now he starts yelling in my ear.

"You son of a bitch."

He's yelling and swearing at me and I'm laughing like hell. He was still cussing and I was still laughing when I hung up the telephone.

4

By now I guess you must have figured out that my all-time favorite character in baseball was Casey Stengel. I loved that man. That's why, wherever I have managed, I have always had a picture of Casey hanging on the wall in my office.

Much of what I am as a manager I took from Casey Stengel. Unfortunately, many people today only remember Stengel for what he did with the New York Mets. That's not fair. He was old then and he did a great job for the Mets as a salesman and ambassador for the game of baseball in general and the Mets in particular. Even at his age—he was in his seventies when he managed the Mets—he was smart enough to get people talking about baseball wherever he went.

The Mets were a terrible team and Casey knew it. He knew they couldn't win, so he tried to make the people forget how bad they were by telling his funny stories and being a character. What's so unfortunate about that is that people forget that when he was younger, he was a brilliant manager. Of course, he had great players with the Yankees, but he knew how to utilize his people. I don't care how great the players are, when a team wins five consecutive world championships, the manager has to be given a lot of credit for avoiding complacency and using his players properly. Five straight world championships is something I don't think you'll ever see any team do again.

So much of what I learned about the game of baseball, and so much of what I have used as a manager, I took from Stengel. I wasn't even aware at the time that I was picking certain things up, but years later, when I was managing, a situation would come up and I'd remember what Casey did and I did the same thing. It might be platooning right-handed hitters against left-handed pitchers, or putting one of my better home run hitters in the leadoff spot, or getting my starting pitcher out and my relief pitcher in at the right time.

So often something Stengel said, or some little move, came back to me when I was managing. He was always talking on the bench, always explaining the moves he was making and why he was making them. I guess a lot of what I picked up stuck with me by the process of osmosis. As a result, I find myself doing the same thing when I'm managing, talking on the bench, explaining my moves, often to no one in particular.

Probably the most important thing I learned from Casey was the handling of players. I'm flattering myself when I say that, because the old man was a master psychologist. There was only one like him.

If somebody messed up, Casey would never say anything to that player directly. Instead, he would speak generally about the play without mentioning names. He always got his message across. Not only would the guy who fouled up know he was being chewed out, but those who were not involved would get an earful and realize they'd better not foul up.

The thing about the old man was that he knew people and how to treat them, and whatever he was doing, it worked. He just knew how to deal with people, how to get them to respond. He benched me once during the 1952 season. I didn't think I deserved to be benched, so I just took a seat down on the other end of the bench, as far away from him as I could get, and sulked.

Everybody was waiting for us to clash, because I was pissed about being benched and my temper was flaring. Then in the seventh inning, I could see out of the corner of my eye that the old man was walking down the dugout, headed in my direction. I knew he was coming down to tell me to go in for defense and I was going to let him have it. But he just wandered over to where I was sitting, stopped in front of me, and said, "Whassa matter? Is widdo Biwwy mad at me?"

That just stopped me. I couldn't yell at him.

"Will you take your widdo gwove and go out and pway second base?" he said.

It was all I could do to keep from cracking up, but that cleared the air and pulled me out of my mood. I never said a word. I just grabbed my glove and headed out to second base. That's how great a psychologist he was.

Funny thing is, when Stengel came to the Yankees as manager in 1949, he was fifty-nine years old. Hell, I was fifty-seven in my last year as manager of the

Yankees, 1985, but for some reason Stengel seemed so much older back then, maybe because he had been out of the big leagues for so long.

He had been a good player with the Brooklyn Dodgers, Pittsburgh Pirates, Philadelphia Phillies, New York Giants and Boston Braves for fourteen seasons, from 1912 through 1925. He was an outfielder with exceptional speed and a lifetime batting average of .284.

He later managed the Braves and Dodgers without much success, never finishing higher than fifth in nine seasons. In the 1942 season, he guided the Braves to a fourth straight seventh-place finish. Just before the 1943 season, Stengel was hit by a car and suffered a broken right leg, which hospitalized him and kept him away from the team for two months. A sports columnist named Dave Egan, writing in the Boston *Record*, said: "The man who did the most for baseball in Boston in 1943 was the motorist who ran Stengel down two days before the opening game and kept him away from the Braves for two months."

Stengel's early managerial career was hardly a distinguished one, and when he was fired by Boston after the 1943 season, it looked like his major league career was over.

But he went back to the minor leagues to manage the Oakland Oaks in the Pacific Coast League, which was where I played for him. Remember, this was just after World War II and major league baseball had not yet expanded to the West Coast. The Pacific Coast League was still hot stuff. Some teams drew even more than some major league teams, and Casey was close to home, so he was content to live out his life as a manager in the Pacific Coast League. He was in his upper fifties, too old to be thinking about another major league job.

But he attracted attention by taking an Oakland team that had been perennial also-rans and finishing second with them in 1946. The following year, the Oaks slipped to fourth. But in 1948, Stengel guided them to a first-place finish and the league championship in the playoff series. It was that success that brought him back to the major leagues as manager of the New York Yankees in 1949 at age fifty-nine. The selection of Stengel to succeed Bucky Harris as manager of the Yankees was a well-kept secret and a shock.

Nobody could have predicted it. There was no connection between Stengel and the Yankees, or with George Weiss, for that matter, except that Weiss was aware of the job Casey had done in Oakland and was sufficiently impressed with it to ask him to manage the Yankees.

The announcement was met with skepticism and scorn, partly because of Stengel's age, partly because he was a proven failure as a major league manager and partly because Casey had a reputation as a buffoon. Stengel never did anything to conceal that reputation. In fact, he often enhanced it with such stunts as coming up to home plate one day and removing his cap to allow a sparrow to fly free. Stengel also was a great storyteller, a nonstop talker who seemed never to be able to remember names. He would keep the sportswriters enthralled with his funny stories, which helped his reputation as a clown, but did nothing to help him gain acceptance as a manager. That would come later, when he won pennant after pennant. In 1949 he won the pennant and the World Series, the first of an unprecedented five consecutive world championships, from 1949 through 1953.

Stengel managed the Yankees for twelve seasons, from 1949 through 1960. He won ten pennants and seven world championships, and I am proud to say I played on seven of those pennant winners and six of those world championship teams.

I can remember just before the 1952 season. We were playing the Brooklyn Dodgers in an exhibition game and Mickey Mantle had never seen the Dodgers' ballpark, Ebbets Field. It had this high wall in right field and center field that kind of jutted out at a sharp angle at the bottom. It was a difficult wall to play because the ball would carom off crazily, but of course Casey was very familiar with the wall, having played there for several years.

So before the game, Stengel took Mickey out to the outfield and began to explain to him how to play the wall, telling Mick how he used to do it. You have to remember, by now Stengel was in his sixties and he had this wrinkled face and these huge elephant ears and this big nose. He was bent over and his right leg had a big knot from where he had been hit by the car in Boston. And Mickey is listening to all of this and looking at Stengel with a funny look on his face, like he couldn't believe what he was hearing.

"You mean you played here?" Mickey said.

"Yeah," said Case. "What do you think, I was born sixty years old?"

Later, when I became a manager, I tried to remember all the things Stengel taught me and I tried to use a lot of the things I had learned from him. The one thing he was always on us about was to think out there on the field. He'd tell us that was our office and we had better concentrate on our job or what's the use of being out there.

"When you're on deck, waiting to hit," he'd say, "it's your job to know how many outs there are, what the score is, what inning, what I might be thinking. You got to be prepared. You got to be ready for anything I might do. I don't want you to go up there just thinking, 'I have to get a hit.' I want you to be thinking up there."

One day he took the whole team out on the field before a game. "This is home plate," he said. "When you come up here, before you come up here, you should know what your job is. You, Martin. You're batting in front of Mantle. Your job is to get on base. Mantle's the home run hitter, not you. Pull your uniform shirt out, get hit with a pitch, whatever you have to do to get on that base. If it's the ninth inning and we're behind, you've got to get on that base. That's your job."

At one point during the 1953 season, Mickey and I were both in a slump. We were striking out a lot and whenever we did, we'd come back to the bench and throw our bats down, kick the water cooler, fling our helmets. Casey called us into his office and tried to talk to us about it.

"Look," he said, "you're going to strike out. It's part of the game. Don't let it get you. Don't lose your cool. Laugh if off and just bear down harder the next time."

So Mickey and I talked it over and we decided that if we struck out, we'd try to laugh it off. Mickey would strike out and he'd come back to the bench. He'd lay his bat down gently, put his helmet down and start laughing.

"Ha, ha, ha, did you see that?" he'd say. "I struck out again. Ha, ha, ha."

And I would strike out and do the same thing.

"Hey, he struck me out. Ha, ha, ha."

Pretty soon, after we'd done that a few times,

Stengel just looked at us and said, "That will be enough of that shit."

I always wished that I could be more like Stengel in the way he was able to deal with people. He was witty and brilliant. He was so much smarter than the people he was talking to that they couldn't understand him and they thought he was a dummy. But he wasn't. He had a strange way of expressing himself, but if you were around him long enough you began to understand what he was saying and he made a lot of sense. He was just brilliant about baseball. He had total recall of things that happened years before.

After I was traded by the Yankees, I was hurt. I felt Stengel could have prevented it. Of course, he couldn't, but I was so hurt I had to blame somebody and I stopped talking to Stengel. I didn't talk to him for five years. I'd be playing against the Yankees and I wouldn't even acknowledge him, wouldn't say hello to him. Or we'd be at a banquet together and I'd go out of my way to avoid him.

I know it hurt Casey, because he kept telling people, "He won't talk to me. The little dago won't talk to me."

It was Mickey Mantle who convinced me I was being a baby. He kept telling me, "Why don't you bury the hatchet? Talk to the old man. He feels so bad because you won't talk to him. He's always asking me about you."

But I was stubborn. I was going with Gretchen at the time. We were engaged to be married. She was an airline hostess and one day Casey got on one of her flights. He found out who she was and now she couldn't get away from him.

"Let me tell you about this kid," he said. "Let me tell you how great he is. Let me tell you . . ."

Gretchen felt like saying to him, "If he's so great, then why did you get rid of him?" But she didn't.

As time went on, I realized that it wasn't Stengel's fault that I got traded. He couldn't help it. He really had no choice. George Weiss had made up his mind to get rid of me and there was nothing Stengel could do. I began to feel bad that we weren't talking. I said to myself, "What the hell are you doing? This man has helped you more than anybody in baseball and if he dies and you haven't made up with him, you'll never forgive yourself."

This is how great he was. I hadn't talked to him for I don't know how many years, and then at the winter baseball meetings in Houston, where I was scouting for the Twins at the time, I see Stengel in the lobby of the hotel, talking to the press. I was going to walk right by him, but I decided to say something because I admired him so much. I figured this had gone far enough. I threw my stubbornness and my ego out the window.

"Hiya, Case, how's everything? How's Edna?"

And he turns to the writers and says, "Let me tell you about this guy. This guy was the greatest . . ."

Like it never happened. After all those years. That's how great Casey Stengel was.

In the end, it was sad. He'd come to the Yankees' Old Timers' Day and he'd come in the clubhouse and all the big guys were there, Mickey and Joe D., but they were so busy they just didn't have any time for him. I knew he was lonely, so I started talking to him.

"How's Edna, Case?"

"Edna's cuckoo," he'd say. "She's lost it, Bill."

Edna Stengel was in a home and she didn't even know Casey. When he died, she didn't even know her husband was dead. But he was devoted to her right up until he died. He'd go to the home every day and wheel her around. Casey had one of those garages with pillars on the side and in the back there was a railroad crossing gate because Casey had gone through the back wall of the garage about three or four times. His car looked like a Sherman tank. It had so many nicks and scratches on the side you'd have thought the guy who drove that car must have been killed.

He wasn't supposed to drive. They had his license taken away because of his age, but he didn't want to walk when he went to visit Edna, so he would drive anyway. The police would see his car weaving on the road and they'd stop him and pick him up.

"You know you're not supposed to drive," the policeman would say, and Casey would mumble something. The policeman never would do anything to him. He'd just take him home and be on the alert for him the next time he took his car out.

Casey finally died without a will. At least, his family claimed he had no will, but I don't believe it. I know he had a will. Nobody knows to this day what happened to all his money.

I went to his funeral and I even slept in his bed the night before the funeral. My girlfriend Jill and I frequently visit his grave in Glendale when we're at home in Southern California in the winter. We leave flowers and we sometimes stand up there on the hill where he's buried and I'll just talk to Jill about him and how much I loved and respected him.

Most of all, I'm happy I swallowed my pride and patched up my feud with him before he died. I would never have forgiven myself if I didn't, because he was, and still is, the most important person in my baseball life.

5

As far back as I can remember I wanted to be a ballplayer. And as far back as I can remember, people kept telling me I was too small to make it. I was always the smallest kid in my class, the smallest on the baseball team, the smallest on the basketball team. It wasn't until I was out of high school that I started to grow. I grew three inches to just about my present height of five-eleven.

One of my earliest memories is of telling my mother I was going to be a ballplayer. We were a poor family, always scratching to make ends meet. We didn't have a refrigerator or even an old-fashioned icebox because we couldn't afford one. Instead, we kept our food in a pantry. Cool air would come up from the basement through an iron grating into the pantry and that's where the food was kept. I remember telling my mother, "Ma, when I become a ballplayer, I'm going to buy you an icebox. I'm going to buy you new furniture. I'm going to buy you a new car."

I guess I was about ten or eleven at the time and I did everything I promised. I bought her four new cars.

About five years later, when I was in high school, I had to do a book report and the book I chose was *Lou Gehrig: A Quiet Hero*, by Frank Graham. That cinched it. That book had a tremendous effect on me. After reading it, I knew I wanted to be a baseball player, and I knew I wanted to be a Yankee.

In a way, it was a good thing I discovered baseball at an early age. I was getting into too many fights in the neighborhood, hanging out with a tough crowd, and who knows what might have become of me if I didn't have baseball, basketball and football to use up so much of my energy. I don't want to get too melodramatic about this, but sports might have saved me from a horrible life.

I was always a pretty good baseball player, but when I was a kid that wasn't even my best sport. I was good enough in basketball so that there was some talk that Santa Clara University was interested in me and might offer me a scholarship. To tell you the truth, football was actually my best sport. I liked football because of the contact. I loved to hit. I never played high school football because my mother refused to sign the parents' consent form, but I played sandlot football without her knowledge. I was a quarterback on offense and a halfback on defense and I could hit hard for a kid who weighed only about 118 or 120 pounds.

But baseball remained my true love. We had a

guy who lived in our neighborhood who was a friend of my older brother. They had been classmates at Berkeley High. The guy's name was Augie Galan and he had a very good major league career with the Chicago Cubs, the Brooklyn Dodgers and the Cincinnati Reds. He played from 1934 through 1949, sixteen seasons in the big leagues. I was just getting into baseball and I was at an impressionable age when Augie was playing in the big leagues and I guess he influenced me as much as anyone. When he came home during the off-season, he would work with me and help me.

We lived on Seventh and Virginia. The Galans owned a laundry on Seventh and San Pablo, which was just four blocks away. I admired Augie so much because he was a major leaguer and we never saw major league baseball out there in California. I would follow the majors through the newspapers. I was still a Yankee fan because of Lou Gehrig, but the Cubs were my second favorite team because of Augie Galan. The walls of my room were covered with Cubs' pictures that Augie had sent me.

There were others in the area who played in the major leagues, like Joe Hatten, a pitcher for the Cubs and Dodgers, who came from Livermore, and Ray Lamanno from Oakland, who was a catcher with the Reds.

The teams I played on as a kid were sponsored by local bakeries and different stores in the neighborhood. Later, I played American Legion ball. But the best time for me to improve was actually during the winter. All the pros were home and every Saturday they would gather at James Kenney Park and play these choose-up games. I was only a little kid at the time, nine or ten or eleven, but I'd go down to the park and hope they would be short a player so they would pick me. It happened a lot. They'd stick me in right field, where I could do the least harm, and I really learned the game and improved by playing against players of that caliber.

This went on for several years. They even formed a Saturday league with teams sponsored by local breweries like Lucky Lager and Ben's Goldie. It was good for the pros because they picked up a little money and they kept in shape all year long and it was good for me because I was playing in fast competition and learning a great deal and improving. The Commissioner of Baseball eventually put a stop to it, which I never could understand, because guys who lived in foreign countries were permitted to play winter ball in their native lands, but guys who lived in the United States were forbidden to do the same thing.

I thought I was getting to be a pretty good player and I was certain that once I graduated from Berkeley High the scouts would come around and I'd be signed to a professional contract. I was the shortstop and cleanup hitter on the school team and I led the team in hitting.

At the same time, I was playing in a league in Oakland on Sundays. The Oakland Oaks of the Pacific Coast League sponsored a team called the Junior Oaks and they invited me to play for them. Red Adams, the trainer for the Oaks, took a liking to me and looked after me. He gave me money for bus fare so I could go from Berkeley to Oakland and he gave me money for a hamburger and a milk shake. Red was very nice to me. So was Eddie Leishman, who was managing in the Oaks farm system.

But when I graduated from Berkeley High, there were no offers. Another player on our team was signed to a contract and I wasn't and that really got me down. Nobody would tell me why I was passed up, but there were hints that the reason was my size. Or lack of it.

I was so discouraged I just hung around the park most of the summer, feeling sorry for myself.

Then I was contacted by an Oakland scout named Jimmy Hole. Eddie Leishman was managing Oakland's Idaho Falls team in the Class D Pioneer League and it seems one of his infielders had broken his arm and he needed a replacement. He remembered me from that winter league with the pros and from the Junior Oaks and he instructed Hole to contact me. I don't think Hole approved, because he didn't even drive me down to Oakland to work out the contract. My older brother ended up driving me to Oakland, where I met with Oaks owner Brick Laws and another scout Cookie DeVincenzo.

"Eddie Leishman wants to have you at Idaho Falls because one of his infielders got hurt," DeVincenzo said. "Do you have a suitcase?"

I told him I didn't.

"Do you have a suit?"

I said I didn't have a suit, either. I had one suit, but my uncle had just died and they buried him in it.

"No," I said. "I don't have anything."

Laws gave me $300, part of which I used to buy a suitcase and a suit and a pair of Levi's jeans. I didn't even own a baseball glove. I borrowed one from the equipment room at the playground and used it for the rest of the season; I returned it when I came home. There was only about six weeks left in the season and I was going to be paid $200 a month with no guarantee that I would have a job after the season was over. It was up to me to prove that I could play pro ball. This was my big chance and I was determined not to blow it.

I reported to Eddie Leishman at Idaho Falls and he put me right in the lineup at third base. The first ball that was hit to me, in the first inning of my first game as a professional, I booted for an error. That was not an auspicious start. Now there was a man on first and the next ball was hit right at me again. I picked it up and threw it to second to start a double play. The ball was foul. I knew it, but I threw it to second anyway. The umpire obviously never saw the ball go foul. He called it fair. So we got a double play on a foul ball in my first game in professional baseball. Would you say that was prophetic?

And that was the first time I learned a valuable lesson: Never take anything for granted in baseball.

I played in thirty-two games for Idaho Falls, came to bat 114 times and had an average of .254 with 7 doubles and 12 RBIs. I didn't exactly set the world on fire, but I did well enough to be invited back for spring training the following season. I reported to camp at Valley of the Moon up in Sonoma and waited for assignment.

The Oaks had two Class C clubs, one in Stockton, which was managed by Johnny Babich, who had pitched briefly in the big leagues. The other was in Phoenix, where Arky Biggs was the player-manager. Stockton was the better of the two and they gave Babich his choice of players. When it came to second basemen, he had to choose between me and a good little player named Eddie Sankoff. He took Sankoff. He didn't want me.

"Nah," he said when they asked him about me. "He ain't gonna make it."

I had wanted to go to Stockton because it was near home, but I wound up in Phoenix instead, playing for Arky Biggs, and that might have been a blessing in disguise. I damn near led the whole United States in hitting that season. I batted .392. I had 230 hits, 48 doubles, 174 runs batted in and 31 stolen bases in 130 games. When I reported to Phoenix, Biggs had me batting eighth in exhibition games. He didn't have any confidence in me at first, but I got five hits in one game and four in another, and by the time the season opened, I was batting fifth. I wound up hitting third or fourth most of the season and leading the league in almost every offensive category.

That was 1947. The next year, I was with the Oakland Oaks of the Pacific Coast League and the manager was the man who would have the greatest influence on my baseball life, Casey Stengel. The New York Giants had tried to buy my contract, but the Oaks kept me and we won the Pacific Coast League championship. I remember Casey used to hit me grounders by the hundreds before every game. He'd hit for hours and I'd stay out there and field them and one day I heard him tell somebody, "That big-nose kid ain't the smoothest fielder I ever saw, but he never gets tired."

Playing for Oakland that year was the best thing that could have happened to me. Not only was it near home and not only did it bring me together with Casey; there were two veteran, former major league stars on that team who taught me so much. Both were natives of Oakland and big local favorites who came to play for the Oaks because their major league careers were over.

One was Ernie Lombardi, "Schnozz" they called him because of his big nose. He was a large bear of a man who was as gentle and warm as he was huge. He had been a truly great player in the major leagues and would eventually be elected to the Hall of Fame. He played seventeen years and had a lifetime batting average of .306, and is the only catcher in baseball history to win two batting titles—.342 for Cincinnati in 1938 and .330 for the Boston Braves in 1942—even though he was so slow he never got a leg hit. But could he hit and throw. He hit the ball so hard and ran so slow that infielders played him back on the outfield grass. Once, when he was playing for the Giants, Lombardi took advantage of that by laying down a bunt. The element of surprise allowed him to beat it out for a hit, and the next day the headline in the New York *Daily News* was: LOMBARDI BEATS OUT BUNT.

The other player was Harry Lavagetto, better known as "Cookie." He played ten years with the Pirates and the Dodgers and is best known for getting one of the most dramatic hits in baseball history. In the fourth game of the 1947 World Series between the Yankees and the Dodgers, a pitcher named Bill Bevens had held the Dodgers hitless for eight and two-thirds innings. There had never been a no-hitter pitched in a World Series game to that point (Don Larsen's perfect game for the Yankees would come nine years later). Lavagetto, a veteran, was sent up as a pinch hitter with two outs and he doubled off the right-field wall in Brooklyn's Ebbets Field for the only hit off Bevens. Two runs scored and the Dodgers won 3–2.

Ironically, neither Bevens nor Lavagetto ever played in another major league game. And Lavagetto wound up back home in Oakland the following year playing for the Oaks, which was a break for me. Lavagetto was an infielder, and a good one, and he kind of took me under his wing. I learned so much from Cookie, who is just a wonderful man.

I batted .277 for the Oaks in 1948 and felt I was ready for the big leagues, but the call never came. Not for me, anyway. It did come for Stengel. The Yankees

shocked the baseball world by making him their manager in 1949 and Casey wound up leading the Yankees
to a world championship, the first of an unprecedented
five straight world championships.

I remained in Oakland and had an outstanding
year—a .286 average for 172 games, 12 homers and 92
RBIs. And the next year, the Yankees bought my contract and the contract of my Oaks teammate Jackie
Jensen, who was from San Francisco and who had been
an all-American football star at the University of California. I knew it was no coincidence that the Yankees
bought me so soon after Stengel got there.

It was an uphill struggle all the way, but I had
made it to the big leagues. I was going to be a Yankee.
Look out, New York.

6

The Yankees bought my contract after the 1949 season on the recommendation of Casey Stengel. Jackie Jensen and I drove from California to St. Petersburg, Florida, for spring training. We stayed at the Soreno Hotel, a big, old, typically Southern hotel with large fans in the lobby and residents whose average age seemed to me to be in the eighties.

When I showed up at Huggins Field, where the Yankees trained, and walked into the clubhouse, I was in awe just looking around the room and seeing all the great stars there. Joe DiMaggio was in one corner, Tommy Henrich in another. I recognized Allie Reynolds and Vic Raschi and Eddie Lopat. The dressing room was small and kind of dilapidated, but this was the big leagues. All the rookies were together in the back of the room and I introduced myself to, and shook hands with, a little blond-haired kid with a funny New York accent who said his name was Eddie Ford.

Some of the players started giving me a hard time at first because I had the reputation of being a wise guy and brash. I had played in the minor leagues with a pitcher named Ralph Buxton, who was in camp that spring, and later heard he kept telling everybody, "Wait till you see this guy Martin. He's a fresh busher."

I had just arrived in camp and already had a reputation to live down. If the truth was known, I was really very shy that first spring, not to mention lonely and homesick. Joe DiMaggio must have realized this, or maybe it was the fact that we were both from Northern California and we were both Italian-Americans. Whatever the reason, he took it upon himself to look after me.

I had been in camp only about a week and I was sitting at my locker when I heard this deep voice say, "Hey, dago, you want to go to dinner tonight?"

I looked up and it was the great DiMaggio. I couldn't believe my eyes and ears. "Yeah, sure, Joe," I said, "I'd like that."

It wasn't anything special. We ate dinner in the hotel dining room and talked about baseball in general and the Yankees in particular. He gave me a pretty good rundown on the probable makeup of the club and what my chances were of sticking, who my competition was and so on. The next thing I knew, I was running with him regularly. Me, a rookie, hanging out with the greatest player in the game.

Joe always would be the last to leave the clubhouse. He took his time getting out of his uniform, showering and dressing, maybe because he was getting older then and he was having physical problems and it took him longer to unwind. Whatever the reason, he'd be the last one out just about every day and I got into the habit of taking my time getting showered and dressed.

He'd say, "Stick around and we'll have a beer." Soon this became a regular routine.

That made the other players jealous. Especially Johnny Lindell and Cliff Mapes. Lindell was a big six-foot-five outfielder from Greeley, Colorado, who also did some pitching in the major leagues. Mapes was almost as big, six-foot-three, but he was just as tough. He was an outfielder from Nebraska.

Lindell and Mapes liked to agitate me. Not really mean, just teasing. I'd be taking batting practice and Lindell would be pitching. He had a good knuckleball and he'd throw me knuckleballs in batting practice to try to make me look bad. Then when it was my turn to throw batting practice, I'd try to knock Lindell on his ass. I'd throw the balls right at him. I didn't care. I was just getting even.

One day I heard Mapes say, "How come that Martin is going out with the big guy? What does Joe see in him?"

And Lindell picked it right up. "Yeah," he said. "Does the punk have something on Joe?"

"You know why Joe is going out with me?" I said. "Because he knows class when he sees it, that's why, you dumb son of a bitch. Joe don't want to hang out with guys with no class." And that would make them madder than hell.

Occasionally the great relief pitcher Joe Page, who also had a reputation of being a pretty good drinker, would join me and DiMaggio. One day Page came with us and he took us to meet his date. The next day our coach, Frank Crosetti, got me alone.

"It's all right you hanging around with DiMag," Crosetti said. "But stay away from that Page."

We broke camp and went North and we opened the season in Boston. I wasn't in the starting lineup, but by the fourth inning we were losing 9–0 and Casey took out most of his starters and put in the subs, figuring the game was lost. The first time I came to bat, there were two men on base and I got my first major league hit, a double off the left-field wall against Mel Parnell that scored two runs.

We continued to bat around, and what do you know, I came to bat again in the same inning and singled in two more runs. I didn't know it at the time, but I had become the first player in baseball history to get two hits in one inning in his first major league game. My record stood for thirty-six years, until it was tied in 1986 by Russ Morman of the Chicago White Sox. But I still feel I hold the record because my two hits came in my first two major league at bats. Morman's were in his second and third at bats.

We wound up winning the game 15 10, and after the game reporters were gathered around DiMag, who had had a big day himself. "Don't talk to me," Joe said. "He's the one you should be talking to." And he was pointing at me.

I continued to hang around with Joe most of that season. I used to root like hell for him because if he had a good day, he'd say, "O.K., kid, we're going out to dinner tonight."

But if he had a bad day, he wouldn't want to go out. We'd just order up and eat in the room and here I was, twenty-two years old and single and I'd be locked up in that room eating dinner with another guy.

Joe roomed alone, the only player we had who did, but it was because he was such a big star. And when we stayed in, we would eat in his room, which was like a small suite.

My roommate that year was Phil Rizzuto and what a nuisance that turned out to be. That was the year Rizzuto won the Most Valuable Player award. He was having a great year and the telephone kept ringing off the hook. It was always for him. Not only couldn't I get any rest, I wound up being Rizzuto's personal answering service.

At one point during the season, Phil got a death threat. Some guy wrote him a letter and said he was going to shoot him during batting practice. Stengel came up with what he thought was the perfect solution. He ordered me and Phil to change uniforms. I was to wear Phil's No. 10 and he was to wear my No. 1, so the guy who sent the letter would be shooting at the wrong player and Phil would be safe. That made me feel great.

We made the switch for about twenty minutes but then Rizzuto changed his mind.

"I'll take my chances on the guy with the gun," he said. "If I wear Martin's number, I'm liable to get hit in the head with a pitch or slugged by one of the players on the other team."

I got to play in only thirty-four games that first season. I batted .250, had 1 homer and 8 RBIs. Jerry Coleman was the regular second baseman and he had a good year, batting .287. We won the American League pennant and beat the Philadelphia Phillies in the World Series in four straight games. I didn't get in a game, but I watched the Series from the bench, just thrilled to be part of it.

After the season, I was drafted into the Army, even though my father had suffered a heart attack and I was supporting seven people. My sisters and my younger brother were in school and my older brother had come out of World War II with stomach problems and was having trouble holding a job. But they drafted me and sent me to Fort Ord and I immediately checked to see if I could get allotments for my family.

I was just a private and they told me, "You don't make enough money to support that many people."

I said I had to have money to support my family and they suggested I go to Officer Candidate School. That interested me until they told me I would have to sign up for another year.

"I'm not signing up for another year," I said. "I've got baseball to go back to."

After a few months, they contacted me and told me they were going to give me a hardship discharge. I didn't want it, but they practically forced it on me. Then when I got the discharge, there was a lot of criticism because I was a ballplayer and people complained and said I was getting preferential treatment. They didn't know that it wasn't even my idea.

As a matter of fact, getting that hardship discharge would backfire on me. I had served a little more than five months. If I had served the full six months, I would have completed my military obligation and would no longer have been eligible for future draft. Instead, I was short of the minimum requirement and I wound up getting drafted a second time, three years later.

I got out of the Army in time to join the Yankees for spring training in 1951. We were training in Phoenix that year, having traded training sites with the New York Giants. I didn't know it at the time, but that would turn out to be Joe DiMaggio's final season in baseball.

I continued to get together with Joe for dinner, but not as often as the previous year. I had my own friends, closer to my age, and Joe was going out less and less because of all the physical problems he was having. There was the old problem of his heel. He had missed most of the 1949 season when he had to have a bone spur removed from his heel. He had to wear a specially built shoe. The heel wasn't his big problem in 1951, but it still bothered him a little.

His big problem in 1951 was his shoulder. He could hardly throw, but we kept it a secret. The other teams never knew it. The infielders would help him out by ranging farther out than normal for relays. His shoulder bothered him all that season and the heel would act up once in a while. He never complained about it, but I could tell.

One of the things I regret about my baseball career is that I never got to see Joe in his prime. He had to be unbelievable. When I played with him, he was at the end of his career and he was still remarkable. What impressed me most about him was his instinct for the game. He would go from first to third as well as anybody I ever saw and he would always make it with ease. I don't ever remember seeing him get thrown out trying to take an extra base, that's how good his instincts were.

The same in the field. He always was off at the crack of the bat and he seemed to have a sixth sense about where the ball would land. He'd get such a great jump on the ball and he'd just seem to be gliding after it, all grace and with such little effort, and he'd be settling under the ball.

He wasn't the hitter in 1950 and 1951 that he had been in his earlier years, but he still was tough in the clutch and he commanded such respect. He got a lot of big hits for us in the two years I saw him.

At the time I knew him, Joe was seeing Marilyn Monroe and I had the privilege of meeting her once. I never went out with them or anything, but Joe introduced me to her during spring training. It was just a brief meeting.

"Hello, how are you?" she said in that soft, sexy voice of hers. She seemed very shy, very polite and very humble. And of course she was beautiful. That was it. I only saw her that one time.

Joe retired after the 1951 season, but I managed to get the last bat he ever used. He used to rub his bats down with a mixture of olive oil and resin to get a good grip. That was before they started using pine tar.

After the final game of the 1951 World Series against the Giants, I saw that bat in the rack and I took it and put it in my locker. Joe saw me take it and he didn't say a thing. In fact, he gave me some other stuff—the specially constructed shoe he wore to protect his heel and some scotch that somebody had given him. I don't have the shoe anymore and I don't know what became of the scotch, but I still have the bat.

A few years ago, I got a call from the Baseball Hall of Fame in Cooperstown asking me if I would donate Joe's last bat to them. I said nothing doing. I had given it to a friend, Louis Figone. Louis and I went to grammar school together and our mothers had grown up together. He lives in El Cerrito, California, now and he has been a loyal and faithful friend for almost fifty years. In fact, Louis owns racehorses and he had a horse recently that he named BillyBall. The horse went on to be named California Horse of the Year.

I gave Louis a bunch of baseball stuff I had, including my MVP trophy from the 1953 World Series, one of my bats, the shoes Joe D. had given me and Joe's last bat. Louis treasures those trophies, but I know that if I ever want them back or want to display them, Louis would return them.

DiMaggio was a lot different then than he is now. Now he's opened up a lot, he's a lot looser, but that's probably because there isn't as much demand on his time as there was when he was a player, and there isn't the constant pressure on him to perform. But I can tell you this. He has always been a super guy as far as I'm concerned, and he still is. He was great to me at a time when I needed somebody to show me some friendship and I will always be grateful to him for it.

People say we'll never see another Joe DiMaggio in our lifetime. I don't know. I don't want to be that pessimistic. After all, when DiMag retired, they said we'd never see another one like him. Then along came Mickey Mantle.

7

The first time I saw Mickey Mantle was in the spring of 1951 in Phoenix, Arizona. As I have mentioned, that year the Yankees traded spring training camps with the New York Giants. They took our camp in St. Petersburg and we took theirs in Phoenix. I never did know why. Probably for the publicity, and to break up the monotony and give the veteran players a change of scenery.

But here we were in Phoenix and we're going through infield drills with Frank Crosetti, the Yankees' third base and infield coach who had been an outstanding shortstop for the Yankees from 1932 until he retired after the 1948 season. He had been the mainstay of the infield on those great teams of Lou Gehrig, Joe DiMaggio and Tony Lazzeri.

Mantle was a shortstop and he was terrible. The previous season, only his second in professional baseball, he had had a sensational year at Joplin, batting .383 to lead the league, with 26 homers and 136 runs batted in. That's the main reason he was in camp that spring. But he also led the league in errors, about 80 of them in 137 games, and when I saw him I could understand why. He could hardly pick up a ball. And when he did, he threw it into the seats.

"Who's that butcher?" I wondered.

When he got in the batting cage, it was a different story. My recollection is that he couldn't have been more than 165 or 170 pounds in those days. But what power. I watched him hit a couple in the seats right-handed. Then he turned around and hit a couple more into the seats left-handed. Now I'm saying, "Who's that little show-off?"

Later, Mickey told me he thought the same thing about me because Crosetti was teaching us how to make the double play and I said to him, "That ain't right."

Crosetti just glared at me with a look that said, "Who do you think you are, you fresh busher?"

But I held my ground. "Cookie Lavagetto taught me this way and Charlie Dressen taught me this way," I said.

As I have mentioned, Lavagetto had come down from the major leagues to play in Oakland when I was there in 1948 and he had spent a lot of time working with me on playing the infield. One of the things he stressed was making the double play and his technique differed from Crosetti's. Later, when Casey Stengel left the Oaks to manage the Yankees in 1949, he was replaced by Dressen, who had also been a major league infielder. Charlie also helped me with the double play and gave me a few other tips, all different from what Crosetti was teaching.

So I'm arguing with Crow about how to play second base and how to make the double play and Mantle's thinking, "Who's this guy Martin trying to tell the great Crosetti about playing second base?"

I wasn't trying to show Crow up. There are more ways than one to make the double play, and I showed him five ways I had learned. When I showed him what Lavagetto and Dressen had taught me, Crow listened and agreed they were effective alternatives, and the next thing you know he had me showing the other infielders.

I didn't spend much time with Mickey that spring. We didn't really have that much in common. He was a shy country boy from Oklahoma and I was this smart-ass city kid from Berkeley. We were on opposite ends of the pole, like we were from different worlds. He might have been from Mars for all I knew. Mars? Oklahoma? Same thing.

He was a funny-looking guy. He wore jeans and plaid shirts most of the time and his blond hair was cut short, it looked like it had been chopped up with a penknife. He had these big forearms like Li'l Abner. In fact, he sounded like Li'l Abner when he talked. Our dress, our speech, our interests—everything about us was different. Still, there was something about him that I liked. And even then I could see the tremendous potential he had as a ballplayer.

We both made the team and went to New York, which brought us a little closer. I had spent some time hanging around with Whitey Ford the previous year, but Whitey was in the Army in 1951 and I was looking for a new running mate. Someone close to my age, like Whitey was.

After about six weeks, Mantle was sent down to Kansas City, the Yankees' AAA farm team in the American Association. He was striking out too much and Casey figured it would be a wise move to send him down to regain his confidence by hitting against pitchers who wouldn't overmatch him. Mickey tore it up in Kansas City and after about six or eight weeks, he was back up with the Yankees. It was then that we decided to room together and that's when we really got to know one another.

It wasn't easy at first. Mickey had these country habits, like getting up at dawn as if he was going to milk the cows or something. I would soon change that. He also liked to listen to country and western music, which I hated.

"How can you listen to that shit-kicking music?" I would tell him.

"Listen to the words," he'd say in that Oklahoma drawl of his. "Just listen to the words carefully and I'll bet you change your mind."

So I started listening to the words and the next thing you know, I was hooked on country music myself. Now I love it. Mickey also got me started wearing cowboy boots. Today that's practically all I ever wear.

That season, we won the pennant by five games over the Cleveland Indians and we played the New York Giants in the World Series. That was the year the Giants came from thirteen and a half games behind the Dodgers in August to tie them and force a three-game playoff, and then the Giants beat the Dodgers on Bobby Thomson's three-run homer in the ninth inning, the so-called "shot heard 'round the world."

We beat the Giants in six games, but not because of any great contribution from me or Mantle. I got in one game as a pinch runner, that's all. But that didn't stop me from cashing the World Series check and spending the money.

Mickey didn't do much better. He went 0 for 3 in the first game and had a single in two times up in the second game. Then, midway in that second game, Mickey was getting under a routine fly ball to right-center (Mantle was playing right, Joe DiMaggio was in center) when suddenly his leg just buckled under him. He went down like he had been shot. I'll never forget it, DiMaggio catching the ball, then looking at Mantle lying at his feet.

They carried Mickey off the field on a stretcher. You could see in his face that he was in agony, and because my roommate was in pain, I was in pain, too. That was the first time we, and the world, found out that Mantle had serious problems with his legs. As a boy, he had osteomyelitis, a bone disease, which they say was the result of an old football injury.

Throughout his career, Mantle would be bothered by problems with his legs. He would play eighteen seasons in the major leagues and he would miss about three hundred games, or the equivalent of two full seasons. Even when he played, he often played with pain in his legs. As great as he was, I can't help wondering how much more he might have done if he had been blessed with good health.

I don't think baseball has ever known a player who had Mantle's combination of power and speed. He was the strongest man, pound for pound, I have ever seen. His power was awesome. Most baseball fans know that from the tremendous home runs he hit. What people don't appreciate is his speed. He may have been the fastest man ever to play this game.

Mantle didn't begin to fill out physically until his second year in the major leagues. When I saw him in the spring of 1952, I couldn't believe my eyes. It looked like he had spent all winter lifting weights. He put on about twenty or twenty-five pounds, all muscle, and he now weighed about 195.

He had forearms like a lumberjack and a thick neck and broad shoulders. And what strength! We'd fool around wrestling and Mickey would say to me, "Get your best hold on me."

I'm pretty strong for a guy my size and I'd get him in a hold and I was sure he'd never get out. But the next thing I knew, I was flying against the wall. I beat him one time. I got behind him and grabbed him by the mouth and held on to his gums so tight he couldn't even close his mouth. Made his gums bleed for a week. It was the only time I ever did beat him wrestling.

I never saw anybody who could run like Mickey. I could run like hell myself. They once clocked me in 3.6 seconds going from home to first, which is faster than Rickey Henderson. But Mickey was clocked in 3.1 seconds from the left side and 3.3 from the right side. That's motoring. No question, he could have been an Olympic sprinter.

I wouldn't dare try to run against him. No way. There was an outfielder around at the time named Jim Busby, who played for Chicago, Washington, Baltimore, Boston, and a couple of other clubs. He wasn't a very good hitter, but he was an outstanding center fielder, mainly because of his speed. Busby could go get them with the best of them. He was from Texas and people were saying he was the fastest player in baseball.

In 1953, he was with the Washington Senators and, naturally, the Yankees were saying Mantle was the fastest player in baseball. So they set up a match race between them one day in Washington as a promotional stunt.

They were to run 100 yards to see who was faster, and the winner was going to get something like $50. Busby set up starting blocks and everything. Evidently, he had done some sprinting in high school or college in Texas. Mickey never did. He just stood there at the start waiting for somebody to tell him when to start running.

They fired a gun and Busby jumped out in front by maybe ten or twelve yards. Don't forget, he was coming out of the blocks. Mickey started slowly because he didn't have traction. Then, all of a sudden, here comes Mantle . . . Buzz-z-z-z. He went by Busby like a train. His last fifteen strides were just unbelievable.

Later, after I was traded, I learned about Mickey's speed firsthand. Mickey would come to bat and look at me playing second base and he would gesture like he was going to drop a bunt.

"Not on me, you're not," I'd say, and I'd move in real close. But he would bunt anyway and he'd still beat it out easily. That's how fast he was. He would tell you he was going to bunt, you would know he was going to bunt, and he'd beat it out even though I was playing so close to him I could practically reach out and touch him, the son of a bitch.

But I got him one day when I was playing for Kansas City. He faked like he was going to bunt and I started moving in real close. Then, all of a sudden, he started laughing and everybody was wondering what the hell was so funny. Mickey was laughing so hard he had to step out of the batter's box. Nobody could see it, but what happened was that I had put my glove on the wrong hand and I started to inch up close to him and when he looked down and saw my glove on my right hand, it just broke him up.

I get a kick at how they always said I led Mantle astray. Did it ever occur to anybody that it might have been the other way around? Mickey never knew how to drink. We'd go out, say, to Danny's Hideaway or the Harwyn Club or one of those places and he wouldn't sip his drink, he'd just gulp it right down, so the next thing you knew, he was feeling pretty good. He'd always carry a lot of money in his pocket, $5,000 or $6,000. This was later, when he began to make big money. He'd get to feeling good and he'd start throwing his money around, $100 tips here, $100 tips there, until he had nothing left.

Sometimes I would want to leave because I was tired, but Mickey would want to stay out, so I'd tell him, "Give me your money."

"Oh, no," he'd protest. "You're not going to do that to me again."

But I'd insist. "Give me your money."

I'd take most of his money and leave him with about $500, and it never failed, the next day I'd see him and the first thing he'd say would be: "Son of a bitch."

"What's the matter?"

"I lost all my money."

"How much?"

"About six thousand dollars."

He had forgotten he'd given it to me and I'd pretend to feel sorry for him.

"Oh, shit," I'd say. "Now what are you going to do?"

I'd let him worry for a while and then put my hand in my pocket and take out his money and hand it to him. Over the years, I probably saved him $300,000.

In recent years, when Mickey was coming to

spring training with the Yankees as a special instructor, George Steinbrenner would pay him a living-out allowance. He'd get it once a week and it usually came to a pretty good package. Most of the time, he wouldn't be there to collect it. He'd be off somewhere playing golf or making a speech or an appearance for George, so I'd collect his money while he was gone and hold it for him, knowing how he threw his money around. But I wouldn't give it to him when he returned because he'd just spend it foolishly and he would forget that I had his money. I'd keep it until spring training was just about over, and when it was time for him to leave, I'd give him the money I had collected for him all at once, about ten packages, maybe as much as $4,000.

"You son of a bitch," he'd say.

"Hey, you got it now, pal," I'd tell him. "You wouldn't have it if I gave it to you a couple of weeks ago."

I mentioned a place called the Harwyn Club. That was a big celebrity hangout in New York in the 1950s and Mickey and I spent a lot of time there. We were getting to be well known in New York and, to tell you the truth, it was a kick to rub elbows with the rich and famous.

On the road, we would hang around with Whitey Ford, too, the three of us running together after Whitey got out of the Army. But Whitey was living on Long Island with his wife, Joanie, and his three kids, and when the team was home, he would rarely get together with us. So it was me and Mickey hanging out at Danny's Hideaway or the Harwyn Club.

The guy who ran the Harwyn Club was a man named Ed Wynne and he got to be a good friend of Mickey's and mine. We even invited him to come hunting with us one winter and he showed up with a Colt .38. We called it his New York rifle.

At the time I really had a thing for Grace Kelly. I thought she was so beautiful. I kept asking Ed if she ever came in the club and he said she did, occasionally. And whenever I went in, I'd always ask him the same thing. "Has Grace Kelly been in?"

And the answer would always be the same. "No."

I had met a lot of celebrities in the Harwyn, but never Grace Kelly, and I told Ed Wynne that if I was in there while Grace Kelly was there, he should let me know. I didn't want to meet her, I just wanted to see her in person.

Sure enough, Mickey and I are in there one night, just the two of us, and we're having a drink. The Harwyn had this special section with booths that sat six people and each booth was separated from the booth next to it by a glass partition. Ed Wynne comes over and says, "Guess who's here tonight."

"Who?" I say.

"Grace Kelly and Prince Rainier of Monaco."

This was before they were married, but their romance was getting a lot of attention in the papers.

"No kidding," I say. "Where are they?"

"Don't look now," he said, "but they're sitting right behind you."

"You've got to be kidding," I said, all excited. "Hey, Mick, she's sitting right behind us."

"Be cool, Billy," Mickey says. "Don't be too obvious."

"I am, I am."

So I play it cool. I grab my drink and I take a sip and slowly I turn my head around to get a look at her. And just as I did, she also turns around and there I was looking her right in the eyes, no more than six inches away. I almost died. I just casually said, "Hello."

And she casually said, "Hello."

Then I turn around quickly and take a big gulp out of my drink. I almost swallowed it glass and all, I was so nervous.

Another night, Mickey and I were in there and sitting across the room was Elizabeth Taylor. She was with Michael Todd, who was her husband at the time, and Rock Hudson. Ed Wynne came over and asked if Mickey and I would pose for a picture with the three of them. We said we'd be glad to.

We went over and Ed makes the introductions all around and, let me tell you, I looked at Elizabeth Taylor's face and it was like looking at the face of an angel. Her features were perfect. She was simply lovely, the most beautiful woman I had ever seen in my life. I just couldn't believe a woman could be that beautiful. And she was wearing a low-cut dress. Oh, my God, I thought I had died and gone to heaven.

So Ed introduces us and she's very nice and sweet although I'm not even sure she knew who we were. And we pose for the picture and that was it, the whole thing took no more than a few minutes. Now Mickey and I return to our table and I just can't get over how beautiful Elizabeth Taylor is. I'm talking a mile a minute.

"Mickey," I said. "Did you see that face? Did you ever see such a face? That is the most beautiful face I have ever seen in my life."

"I ain't seen her face," Mickey said, "but did you see them tits?"

8

People wonder whether it bothered me because other Yankees got all the attention whenever we went anywhere, but I can honestly say I never resented it. I was used to being overshadowed by DiMaggio, Phil Rizzuto, Yogi Berra, Mantle, Whitey Ford and all the other great players the Yankees had in those years. I had no resentment at all.

We'd go to the World Series and the newspapers would always compare the two teams, position by position. Except for my one pinch-running appearance in 1951, I played in four World Series and each one was against the Brooklyn Dodgers, in 1952, 1953, 1955 and 1956. I would be compared with Jackie Robinson or Jim

Gilliam and the papers would always give the Dodgers a big edge at second base.

Robinson was the Dodgers' second baseman in 1952. He batted .308 for the season compared to my .267. But in the Series, Jackie hit .174 and had 2 RBIs; I batted .217 and had 4 RBIs. Edge Martin.

By 1953, Robinson had moved off second base and Gilliam was the Dodgers' regular there. And every year he would outhit me and the papers would give the Dodgers the edge at second base. But in every World Series, I outhit Gilliam—.500 to .296 in 1953; .320 to .292 in 1955; .296 to .083 in 1956.

At the World Series the photographers would be on the field before the game, taking pictures of Joe D., Mickey, Whitey, Yogi, Hank Bauer, Gene Woodling and Gil McDougald and ignoring me. Before the opening game of the 1953 Series, they were doing the same thing and I said to them, "Hey, you'd better take my picture because I'm going to be the star of this thing."

The photographers would look at me and laugh.

"We don't need you, Billy."

"O.K.," I'd say, "Go ahead and leave me out. But you're going to come looking for me to take my picture and I'm going to be too busy."

And sure enough, that was the year I set a World Series record for hits in a six-game series with twelve. The year before I had made the catch of Jackie Robinson's pop fly with the bases loaded in the eighth inning. I'm sure you have seen the pictures. My hat has flown off and I'm catching the ball below my knees, just before it hits the ground. When the ball was popped up, I thought it was the first baseman's play. But apparently he didn't see it. Nobody was moving, so I just took off and the wind kept blowing it back toward the stands and I kept running after it. It seemed the harder I ran, the more the wind took it. I came from almost back on the outfield grass and finally caught up with it between the pitcher's mound and the third base foul line, just as it was about to drop.

Later, our lovable general manager, George Weiss, said, "It was an easy play. Martin only made it look hard."

Yeah! Right! Thanks for the nice words, Mr. Weiss.

The funny thing about my career was that they didn't count game-winning RBIs in those days, but if they did I bet I would have been at or near the top in the league in that category almost every year. So many times I'd get the big hit to win the pennant or the World Series, but no credit. As long as we won, it never bothered me.

Although I dreamed about playing in the major leagues and the Yankees were my favorite team, once I started playing professionally, I never cared if I became a Yankee or not. I was happy playing in Oakland, playing close to home, making good money, a hero in my own home area. When the Oaks sold me to the Yankees, I wasn't exactly thrilled with the idea. Especially when I found out I would have to take a cut in pay. I had earned $9,000 in Oakland in 1949, but when I got to the Yankees, the most George Weiss would give me was $7,500. Can you imagine? I was going from the minor leagues to the major leagues and I was getting a pay cut. When I complained to Weiss, he said not to forget that I had a good chance of getting a World Series share, which was true. My first year with the Yankees, my salary was $7,500 and my World Series check was $6,400.

When I got to New York everybody said I

wasn't the Yankee type. George Weiss blamed everything that went wrong on me. He said I was a bad
influence, that I wasn't the Yankee type. Not the Yankee
type? What is the Yankee type? I always thought it was a
guy who wanted to win and would do anything to win.
What is Yankee tradition? I always thought Yankee tradition was winning.

I remember my first season as a Yankee. Midway in the season, I replaced Jerry Coleman at second
base and we won a game in Cleveland when I hit a
three-run homer. A few days later, I hit a pinch single in
the tenth to beat the St. Louis Browns. The next day,
Stengel told me I was being sent down to Kansas City. I
was disappointed, but I tried not to show it.

"Ain't ya mad?" Stengel said.

"Yeah, I'm mad," I said.

"Well, then why don'tcha go up there and tell
Weiss off?"

And that's just what I did. I went right up to
the front office and gave George Weiss a piece of my
mind, which I'm sure didn't put me on the top of his
Christmas list. I think that's what Stengel wanted me to
do. He wanted me to tell Weiss off because he was
feuding with him and that was his way of getting back
at him. But I don't think Weiss ever forgot or forgave
me for telling him off. It took him seven years to get rid
of me, but I believe he sat and waited for the chance to
get me out of there.

I spent thirty days in Kansas City in 1950, then
came back and was with the Yankees to stay. In 1951, I
got in only 51 games. In 1952, I played in 109 games. It
wasn't until 1953 that I became a regular, playing in
149 games and being named the Most Valuable Player
in the World Series. I was at the peak of my career.
Wouldn't you know it? In the prime of my career, at the

top of my game, I was drafted into the Army for the second time.

The call came just a few months before I would have been over age. And, of course, the fact that I was given a hardship discharge earlier was coming back to haunt me. If I had served another few weeks back then, I wouldn't have been eligible for the draft this time. Also, at that time there was a lot of controversy about professional ballplayers, and other celebrities, getting favorable treatment from their draft boards. The fact that I was a World Series hero, with the spotlight on me, made me vulnerable.

My younger brother Jackie volunteered for the Army because he couldn't get a job. Nobody would hire him because he was draft age, so he figured he might as well enlist. The Army rejected him, but they took me a second time. With seven dependents.

I almost got myself court-martialed in the Army for not standing in line to collect my pay. What happened was, I had so many allotments being taken out of my pay that all I had coming to me was $8 a month. So I said screw it, I'm not going to stand in line for a lousy $8, and the captain wanted to court-martial me because I refused to stand in line.

I had reached the rank of corporal and in my last week they wanted to make me a sergeant, but I refused. Who needed it then? They also wanted to give me an early release. Again, I refused. I figured I was going to serve my full term so nobody would say I got any favors because I was a ballplayer. So I put in my time and when I was discharged I even got a good conduct medal. Now there's one for the books. "Bad Boy" Billy Martin with a good conduct medal from the U.S. Army. Who would ever believe that? But it's true.

It's right there on my discharge papers. As Casey Stengel used to say, you could look it up.

I came back for the tail end of the 1955 season. We won another pennant. In 1956, I got my old job back and we won another world championship.

You might think it merely a coincidence, but in the first four years I was a Yankee, even for part of the season, we won four pennants and four world championships. Is this another coincidence? In 1954 I missed the entire season because I was in the Army. That year, the Yankees finished second. Then I came back and we won two pennants and another world championship. Seven seasons, or parts of them, with the Yankees. Seven pennants. Six world championships. Although I didn't play in the 1950 and 1957 World Series. In 1950, I was a backup player. In 1957, I was gone.

It was because of the Copacabana Incident. I'm sure you have heard about the Copa Incident. It was in all the papers. But you probably heard it all wrong. This is the truth. This is exactly what happened that night.

It was my twenty-ninth birthday, May 16, 1957, and it so happened we had a day off the following day, so we decided to go out on the town to celebrate my birthday. There were five couples and me. I didn't have a date. There was Mickey Mantle and his wife, Whitey Ford and his wife, Hank Bauer, Yogi Berra and Johnny Kucks and their wives. We went to dinner, then we decided it was early, so we'd go to the famous Copacabana nightclub to see Sammy Davis, Jr., who was headlining the show there.

They put us in the back and we were having a good time and all of a sudden, Bauer nudges me.

"See those five guys there?" he says, pointing at a group of tough-looking guys at another table.

"They're looking for trouble. One of those guys has been giving me a bad time."

It turned out that the guys were also giving Sammy Davis a hard time, making all kinds of racial remarks. There were some words and the next thing I knew, we were going outside to see if we could straighten out the mess.

One of the guys comes over to me and I figured there was going to be trouble. But in a nice, polite, calm voice, he asked me to go into the hall. "Look," he said, "my brother and your friend [Bauer] have been going at it all night. We have to keep them apart."

I told him that was fine, that I certainly agreed. We didn't want any trouble. Being major league ballplayers, and especially Yankees, we couldn't afford to get into a fight. I knew that if we did, it would be smeared all over the newspapers.

While we were talking, we heard a loud noise from the next room. The brother and I ran into the room and there was this guy lying on the floor. It was the brother of the fellow I was talking with.

Just then, Mantle comes in, pushes me and the other guy away, looks at this guy lying on the floor and shouts, "Billy!"

Mickey thought it was me because the guy was lying face down.

"Mickey," I said. "Here I am. I'm all right."

Until the brother and I walked into the room and saw this guy lying on the floor, I hadn't so much as set eyes on the man. I never did see who hit him or anything else.

We all left right after that. One of the bouncers in the club hustled us out through the kitchen because we were trying to avoid publicity. It didn't work. The next day it was in all the newspapers. I don't know who tipped them off, but later I heard that all the newspapers had tipsters at most of the big restaurants and nightclubs in town just for this reason. And that's how it happened. The tip might have come from a waiter or a busboy or a men's-room attendant or a hat-check girl. It could have come from anywhere.

Anyway, it was blown up out of proportion the next day and naturally George Weiss was steaming. Just as naturally, he blamed me. I didn't hit the guy. I was nowhere near him. But I got blamed.

When I told Mr. Weiss my side of the story, he didn't believe me. He never liked me and he was trying to get rid of me anyway, and now he had the perfect excuse.

Casey tried to protect me, but he couldn't do it. It took Weiss a month, until the trading deadline on June 15, but he finally got rid of me.

Coleman hadn't been playing and as the trading deadline approached, he was getting more and more nervous. He was scared to death he would be traded, especially since we had an excess of infielders.

"I guess I'm going to be gone," he kept telling me.

Then, on June 15, he was really nervous. He was certain his days as a Yankee were over.

"There's only one way to find out," I told him. "Go out and look at the lineup card. If your name is on there, I'm gone."

I had driven in two runs the day before, which means I could expect to be in the lineup again. But I had a premonition and I was right. Coleman's name was on the lineup card at second base.

It was a no-no to sit in the bullpen during a game. You had to sit in the dugout. But I was so disgusted I couldn't sit in the dugout and when the game started I went right down to the bullpen so I would be out of sight. Along about the seventh inning, here comes Stengel walking down there.

"Billy, can I talk to you?"

I followed the old man into the clubhouse, and Arnold Johnson, the owner of the Kansas City club, came in a few moments later.

Casey is talking to me and he's having trouble getting the words out. He couldn't even look me in the eye. But I knew what was coming.

"Billy," he said, "you're going to Kansas City . . . I couldn't . . . Mr. Johnson, let me tell you about this kid, he's one of the best . . ."

"You don't have to say nothing," I barked at Casey, cutting him off sharply. "I'll play for you, Mr. Johnson. I won't dog it on you."

I was crying. Mantle came over to me later and he was crying. Ford started crying. We got on the team bus to go back to the hotel and everybody on the bus was real quiet. They all knew. I saw Bobby Richardson sitting by himself, so I slipped into the seat next to him and said, "You're going to be the second baseman now, son. Carry on the tradition."

Bobby thanked me.

I didn't sleep a wink that night. Mickey, Whitey and I stayed out all night and most of the time we were in tears. The next day I came to the ballpark and it felt strange. After all those years, I had to go to the other side. They had to send my clothes over from the Yankee clubhouse and I sent word to the Yankee trainer, Gus Mauch, to send me something for my eyes because I hadn't slept.

When I came to bat, it really felt strange. One day I'm playing for the Yankees, and the next day I'm playing against them. Johnny Kucks was pitching and the first time up I hit a shot off the left-field wall. Yogi was playing left field and he made a hell of a play to hold me to a single.

Then I came up in about the seventh inning with a man on and I hit a home run that put Kansas City ahead. But I had no feeling at all. You're supposed to be happy when you hit a home run that puts your team ahead. Not this time. I went around the bases and I felt absolutely nothing. It was like I was in a daze. I felt more like a traitor than anything else.

The thing that hurt most, even more than taking off the pinstripes and going to a second-division team, was leaving my good friends, especially Mickey and Whitey. What great times we had together and I'm happy to say we still have as close a friendship today as we did when we were teammates.

Whitey's beautiful. As a player, nothing ever bothered him. He never had an ego. He's just a terrific guy, and he was a great pitcher. If you had to win one game, you wanted Whitey pitching for you. If he messed up and lost a game, you'd never hear him complain, you'd never hear him alibi, you'd never hear him blame anybody else for losing. He'd just say, "Hey, I screwed up. I'll get them next time." And he usually did.

Whitey and Mickey are like brothers to me. I always said I wanted to buy the house where Mickey was born and grew up in Oklahoma. This little, old, dilapidated wood house. I want to buy it and turn it into a Mickey Mantle Museum. One of these days, when I am financially stable, I'll do it.

To this day, we still get together and tear it up for old times. There's one thing that bothers me, though. People say I was a bad influence on Mickey and Whitey. But both of them are in the Hall of Fame and I'm not. Maybe I was a better influence on them than they were on me.

9

I never wanted to be a manager. I certainly never planned it, but you come to learn not to plan on anything when you're a professional ballplayer. Managing was the furthest thing from my mind when I was a player.

Something went out of me when the Yankees traded me. Leaving New York, leaving all my closest friends, leaving the pinstripes. Baseball just didn't seem to be the same to me anymore. It didn't seem very important. The great desire I had, the pride I had, seemed to leave as soon as I was traded. I still played hard and had a few pretty good seasons, but somehow it just didn't seem the same. Part of my heart was gone.

With the Yankees, every game you played, every base hit you got, every ground ball you picked up, was important because it was New York and because we were always fighting for a pennant. You had the feeling you were contributing to something. Once I left the Yankees, I never had that feeling.

I finished out the 1957 season in Kansas City, and actually hit better for the Athletics than I had for the Yankees: .257 in seventy-three games for Kansas City, .241 in forty-three games for the Yankees; 9 home runs for KC, 1 for the Yankees; 27 RBIs for the Athletics, 12 for the Yankees. The Yankees won the pennant without me. Kansas City (I can't even bring myself to say "we") finished seventh. I wasn't accustomed to finishing seventh. I had never finished seventh before.

After that season, I was traded again. The Athletics sent me, pitchers Maury McDermott and Tom Morgan, catcher Tim Thompson and outfielders Lou Skizas and Gus Zernial to the Detroit Tigers for pitchers Duke Maas and John Tsitouris, catcher Frank House, first basemen Kent Hadley and Jim McManus and outfielders Bill Tuttle and Jim Small.

I had another decent year in Detroit. Batted .255 and had 7 homers and 42 RBIs. The Yankees won another pennant that year (another World Series check I would have had). The Tigers finished fifth. At least I was moving up in the standings. I was also moving east. When the season ended, I was traded to Cleveland (this was getting to be a habit). A pitcher named Al Cicotte and I went to the Indians for pitchers Don Mossi and Ray Narleski and infielder Ossie Alvarez. I batted .260 for the Indians with 9 homers and 24 RBIs in only seventy-three games. I was hurt a lot that year.

The Yankees didn't win the pennant that season. They finished third. We finished ahead of the Yankees, but it gave me no consolation to beat out the

Yankees by finishing second. The Chicago White Sox
won the American League pennant.

After that season, I was sent to the Cincinnati
Reds with pitcher Cal McLish and first baseman Gordy
Coleman for second baseman Johnny Temple. It was
the first time I had ever been in the National League
and I hardly left my mark. I batted .246 in 103 games,
but hit only 3 homers and drove in only 16 runs. After
that season—you guessed it—I was on the move again
(this was getting monotonous). This time I was sold to
the Milwaukee Braves, my sixth team in six seasons.
After six games, I was traded to Minnesota for infielder
Billy Consolo and it was like going home. It wasn't the
Yankees, but it was the American League, and I re-
sponded with a good season—108 games, 6 homers, 36
RBIs, a .246 average. Good enough, I believed, to war-
rant coming back for another season. I was past thirty
and I knew my career was coming to an end, but I
figured I could still play for another two or three years.
The Twins had other ideas.

Howard Fox, who was the team's traveling secretary, talked Calvin Griffith into releasing me after
that season. I couldn't understand it. I felt I could play
and still produce and I was making $24,000, the most I
ever made as a player. Maybe it was strictly economics,
because to replace me, the Twins brought up Bernie
Allen, who made only $7,000. I was hurt because I
could have used the money. Baseball is funny. Or it was
in my playing days. You got paid the most when you had
lost most of your skills.

Ending my playing career with the Twins may
have been a blessing or it may have been a curse. One
thing is certain: It mapped my future. I had been with
the Twins only that one season, but Griffith had taken a
liking to me. Possibly to soften the blow of releasing me,

he offered me a job as a scout. I didn't have any other prospects at the time and I was pretty sure I wanted to stay in baseball in some capacity, so I took it. I don't know what I would have done if I didn't take the Twins' job. I had no other skills, no schooling. I wasn't prepared to do anything else.

I really enjoyed the scouting job. Just enough traveling, no pressure on you to win and I was close to the game I loved. Later, I would realize that my scouting job helped me as a manager because it honed my ability to evaluate players. I scouted for three years. Then, in 1965, Sam Mele, who was managing the Twins, asked me to be his third base coach. I didn't want to give up the scouting job, but I accepted because of Sam. He had been my manager for most of the one season I played for the Twins and I enjoyed playing for him. I came to like and respect him. So when he asked me to be his third base coach, I couldn't refuse.

The first few weeks I was there, I ran a couple of players into outs at home plate. I was trying to be aggressive, to get the players to be aggressive, and it backfired. I was new on the job and still learning to gauge the speed of our runners—not to mention the strength and accuracy of the opposing outfielders' throwing arms. Naturally, when you gamble, you're going to lose sometimes. But you're going to win more than you lose and you have nothing to gain by being conservative. I have always tried to instill that in my third base coaches. I'd rather see them take a chance and lose than have them sit back passively. Baseball is not a game you can play passively.

Nevertheless, after I ran a couple of players into outs at home plate, I found out that some members of the front office complained to Mele and wanted him to fire me. I never found out who they were and Sam never told me. I didn't want to know. But the Twins were a family business and everybody had something to say about something. The important thing is that it wasn't Sam who was being critical and it wasn't the owner, Calvin Griffith. That's all that mattered to me.

It also mattered that Mele told me about it. He said to these people, "Don't you realize what he's doing? He's forcing them to run. He wants them to be aggressive. He's coaching just the way I want him to."

His real name is Sabath Anthony Mele, but everybody calls him Sam. He's a native New Yorker who had been a star baseball and basketball player at New York University. He was a journeyman outfielder who played for ten years with six different clubs in the 1940s and 1950s. Not a great player, but a good one. His lifetime average was .267 and he hit 80 career home runs with a high of 16 in 1952.

Sam is a big, tough-looking man with a pock-marked face, but he has this soft voice that seems strange coming out of such a big body. He almost purrs when he talks, which meant that as soon as he opened his mouth, his tough-guy image was destroyed.

He called me into his office one day, sat me down and told me softly, "Don't listen to anybody, Billy. Don't pay any attention to all that criticism. I know what you're doing and I agree with you. You just keep right on doing what you're doing. Don't worry about anybody."

I felt much better after talking to Sam and I appreciated his support. After that, I kept getting more aggressive and it paid off. We had a terrific team that year. Four of our guys hit more than 20 home runs. Tony Oliva won the batting title with a .321 average. Zoilo Versalles, our shortstop, batted .273, had 19 homers and 77 RBIs, played brilliantly in the field and was named the American League's Most Valuable Player. Mudcat Grant led our pitching staff with 21 victories, the most in the league. Jim Kaat won 18. We also had Camilo Pascual, Jim Perry and Dave Boswell. And Al Worthington did a great job as our bullpen stopper.

After my talk with Mele, I kept getting more aggressive and it paid off. We won a lot of ball games with aggressive base running and by taking chances. We wound up winning 102 games and the pennant by seven games over the Chicago White Sox. I felt that as third base coach, I contributed to our success with my coaching and by working with our infielders.

Coaching under Mele helped prepare me for the job of managing. One thing he taught me was patience. Sam was another of those low-key, let-them-play type of managers. Another important thing I learned was not to believe everything you hear.

Baseball people are funny as far as sticking someone with a reputation and having that reputation follow the person for the rest of his career. Baseball people have a habit of making knee-jerk conclusions. One guy says something like "So-and-so is a trouble-maker" and the next thing you know, it goes around the baseball grapevine. It's practically impossible to shake that reputation or change someone's opinion of you. I know about such things. Do I ever know about them!

To this day, things I did years and years ago still haunt me and people have preconceived ideas about me. The Copacabana Incident, for example. Here it is more than thirty years later and people are still mentioning it to me.

Baseball people are like women gossiping over the backyard fence. One guy says something and the next thing you know, fifty guys are saying the same thing. Fifty guys say it, then three hundred guys are saying it. Pretty soon, it's accepted as fact.

That goes for things that happen off the field as well as on the field. Reputations that are formed early have a tendency to stick with a player forever.

Gene Woodling got the reputation that he couldn't hit left-handers. Why? Because Casey Stengel platooned him and Gene played mostly against right-handed pitchers. But Casey platooned for the good of the team, to get the maximum out of Woodling's ability. And, of course, he had a hitter like Hank Bauer around to hit against left-handers. It didn't matter. Woodling still had the reputation that he couldn't hit left-handers, and it followed him for his entire career.

That career, by the way, lasted seventeen seasons and continued for eight years and with four more teams after he left the Yankees. Gene had a lifetime batting average of .284 and he had 1,585 hits in his career, so he must have had some of them against left-handers. No matter. He had a reputation that he couldn't hit left-handers and it was going to follow him forever.

Even worse than having a knock against your playing ability is getting a reputation about your attitude, your courage or your lifestyle. Those kinds of things can almost never be eradicated. That's what happened to a young player we had when I was coaching the Twins. The kid's name was Rodney Cline Carew. He had been born in Panama, but he grew up in New York City. He was a quiet kid, very shy, almost suspicious and with a chip on his shoulder. He was just a skinny kid, but he could swing the bat.

Carew had spent a little more than two seasons in the minor leagues when he came to training camp with the Twins in 1967. I don't know why, but for some reason I took a liking to him and he to me. Since he was a second baseman, and I was in charge of the infielders, I spent a lot of time working with him that spring. And I found him to be not only a great hitter but a kid who could run like a deer, who was willing to learn and who took instruction beautifully. I also found him to be a very sensitive kid, but one of great compassion and feeling, not to mention his burning desire and drive to be the best.

Late that spring, we were having one of those meetings in which you evaluate your team and try to decide who you're going to keep and who you're going to send down. All the coaches were there and the manager and the front office people, like the general manager, the scouts and the farm director and his staff. When Carew's name came up, everybody agreed that the kid had talent, but somebody mentioned that he was a troublemaker and he could be a bad influence on the ball club.

Apparently, Rod had gotten into an argument with his manager in Class A and the manager had sent in a bad report on him. Right away, that made him insubordinate and rebellious and a troublemaker. I listened to all this and I couldn't believe they were talking about the same kid I had been working with. I tried to speak in his behalf, but I was talked down, so I kept quiet and later I went to Mele.

"Sam," I said. "This is a good kid, believe me. He's polite. He comes from a good family. He's quiet. And he works hard."

"Yeah, Billy," Mele said. "But I'm not sure he's ready to play in the big leagues."

"I know the kid, Sam," I said. "I've been working with him. He's ready."

"O.K., Billy," Sam said. "That's good enough for me. We'll play him."

And that's how Rod Carew got his start. I don't have to tell you what he did with the opportunity. Seven batting titles. Over 3,000 hits. One of the truly great hitters to play the game.

The one year I managed him, Carew batted .332 and won his first batting title. He also tied Pete Reiser's major league record by stealing home seven times. I managed Rodney only that one year, but I remained close to him and his wife, Marilyn. And they honored me by asking me to be the godfather to their daughter.

I'm not saying Rodney wouldn't have had a great career if I hadn't spoken up for him that day in 1967. I'm merely trying to point out how reputations start. And that very often those reputations are undeserved. Carew not only became an All-Star and a great hitter; he became one of the most respected players in the game, both on and off the field.

I was happy coaching third base for Sam Mele. At this point, I still had not given any thought to managing, but when we got off to a slow start in 1966, there were stories in the papers that I would be the next manager of the Twins; that Mele would be fired and I would take his job. That hurt me because Sam was my friend. I didn't want him to think I was planting those stories or that I was looking for his job. I wasn't. Managing was the furthest thing from my mind at that time.

Then we began to play better and we spurted at the end of the season, passed a couple of teams and finished second to the Baltimore Orioles. When we won on the final day of the season and clinched second place, I was so happy you would have thought we had won another pennant.

"What are you so happy about?" Mele asked me. "We didn't win."

"Yeah," I said. "But we finished second, Sam. Now they can't fire you."

And that's how I felt about Sam Mele.

Unfortunately, Sam was fired after 50 games of the 1967 season. We had gone from pennant winners in 1965 to second place in 1966 and we got off to a terrible start in 1967. After 50 games, we were 25–25 and in sixth place. All season there had been rumors that Sam would be fired and I would take his place. But the ax finally fell. I didn't want the job and I didn't get it. Instead, they gave it to Cal Ermer and that was fine with me. I felt he deserved the chance.

Calvin Coolidge Ermer had played in only one game in his major league career. He was a long, lean and lanky Southerner who was a career minor leaguer. When he came up to manage the Twins, he was in his mid-forties and he had spent about fifteen years managing in the minor leagues for the Twins. The Twins felt it was only right that Ermer be rewarded for his years of loyalty to the organization, and I agreed.

One of the things in Ermer's favor was that most of the Twins players who had come through the organization had played for him at one level or another. He was familiar with most of our team and he had been successful with them in the minor leagues.

The main reason I had been passed up was that I had no managerial experience. I understood that and I had no argument with it.

The following year, in May, I was asked to go to Denver to replace Johnny Goryl as manager of our Pacific Coast League team, which had gotten off to a horrible start.

I was afraid this was a one-way ticket to obliv-

ion. You know, out of sight, out of mind. What if I went
down there and failed? Would I ever get back to the
major leagues? Also, I was concerned about the security
of my family. There was my daughter by my first marriage, and my son, Billy Joe, was still a baby.

The night before I was to give the Twins my
answer, my wife, Gretchen, and I went out to dinner
with Sherry Robertson and his family. Sherry had
played ten years in the majors with the Washington
Senators and Philadelphia Athletics in the 1940s and
1950s. He was Calvin Griffith's brother and he was part
of the clan who worked for the Twins. Sherry was a
good guy and a good friend and I knew he was in my
corner. He kept telling me to go to Denver and I kept
saying, "No, no, no." I told him of my fears that I might
get lost in the minor leagues and never come back and
he kept telling me that was nonsense and urging me to
take the Denver job.

Gretchen also urged me to go to Denver. We
had been married for nine years at the time and she
may have known me better than I knew myself. She
helped talk me into taking the job.

"Billy," she said, "you're frustrated as a coach.
I can see it when you come home after the team has
lost. You're frustrated because you can't do anything to
directly influence the winning of a game. Down deep,
you really want to be a manager. And you're going to be
a great one. Go to Denver. Prove you can manage.
Prove it to yourself and to everyone else. If you don't
take this opportunity, another one may never come
along and you'll never know if you can be any good as a
manager. You'll never be happy if you don't at least try
it."

Gretchen was right. So was Sherry. They both
opened my eyes. When I went to bed that night, I

couldn't sleep; I kept weighing the pros and cons. I went to bed certain I was not going to take the job in Denver and when I got up the next morning my mind was made up that I was going. And I think that shocked everybody, including Calvin Griffith, when I told him I would go to Denver.

If it hadn't been for Sherry Robertson and Gretchen, I might not have taken the Denver job and my life certainly would have been a lot different.

I went to Denver determined to succeed. Now that I was a manager, I was going to be the best manager I could be.

10

I went to Denver and all of a sudden managing just seemed to come natural to me. Gretchen was right. It was as if I had been managing a baseball team all my life; as if I was born to be a manager. I found I had more patience than I thought I would have. I found that the thrill of victory was even more exciting as a manager than as a player. I learned how much I enjoyed outmaneuvering the guy in the other dugout, how much I enjoyed watching my team execute something I had taught them, how much I enjoyed watching my players learn and improve. I had never had such a high, even as a player. I guess you could say I was hooked on managing.

There was something else I learned at Denver:

Managers should manage in the minor leagues before they go to the big leagues. You learn how to deal with players. Everything that will come up in the major leagues, on and off the field, will come up in the minors, where you can make your mistakes without it hurting so much and without every move you make being magnified because you are in a fishbowl. When you have managed in the minor leagues, you are ready for just about anything if and when the opportunity comes along to manage in the major leagues.

When I arrived in Denver, the team was in last place with a record of 7–22, but I could tell right away that the team had more talent than that and it should have been doing better.

The nucleus of the ball club was four guys who had gone to college, including Graig Nettles, who would be with me later with the Twins and the Yankees. The others were Ron Theobald, a little second baseman who later played with Milwaukee, Joe Solomine, an outfielder, and a big, slow first baseman named Jim Mooring. I had the feeling that these four guys thought they were smarter than everybody else. They were good players, but they had a tendency to think too much instead of doing things instinctively, and they made stupid mistakes.

The first night I arrived, I had the obligatory team meeting, which was a combination "Rah-rah, you-can-do-it," and a kick-ass session. I told them they were better than their record and that I heard they had been acting like they were on vacation and this was a country club (I made that up). I said I was going to work them hard, drive them, but that their reward would be victories.

One of the first things I did when I got to Denver was bench the four college players. All of them.

All at once. I was making a statement. As I knew they would, they came to me and asked me why they weren't playing.

"Because," I said, "you are four dummies. I know you all went to college and I didn't, but you are what I call intellectual stoops. I want you to sit down next to me in the dugout and learn this game from a dummy. Me. So that you will become a smart dummy."

After about four innings of sitting, Nettles came to me and said, "Any chance of getting in there, Skip? I'm getting tired of this shit."

Years later, when we were together with the Yankees, Nettles finally confessed and told me what he thought about me back there in Denver.

"I hated you when you first came," he said. "I didn't like the way you talked, I didn't like the way you acted, I didn't like the way you walked around. I thought you were a regular slave driver."

I had made my point and now my four college players were ready to play, and to listen and learn. They were ready to do things my way. You could just see the change in them. They were graduating. I told Mooring, our lumbering first baseman, "You're going to steal home."

He was one of the slowest players on the team. He thought I was crazy.

"Me?" he said. "Steal home?"

"Yeah, you," I said.

And he did. Stole home twice. He couldn't believe it himself. I had made a point. You don't have to have great speed to steal home. You steal home by learning the habits of the pitcher, by getting the proper lead, by having the instincts to go at the right moment and by employing the element of surprise.

"See how easy it is?" I said.

All of a sudden, managing became fun. I took a team that had won only 7 and lost 22 and we wound up winning 65 and losing 50 for the remainder of the season. These kids did it, I didn't. They listened. And they learned. They didn't know how to win when I got there, but by the end of the season they had learned how to win. And that made baseball fun for them. And that's what I have tried to teach everywhere I've managed. Baseball is fun. Winning is fun.

That, I suppose, is one of my basic philosophies of managing—that winning is fun. Another philosophy is this: Be honest with the players and let them be men. If I show my players loyalty, they'll give me loyalty in return.

Nettles again: "After I got to know you and understood what you were trying to do, I changed my opinion. I no longer disliked you. I liked winning and I could see that all you were doing was trying to get us to learn how to win. Then I enjoyed playing for you."

Like I said. Winning is fun.

A manager's biggest job is actually done before and after a game. Let's face it, most people who become managers have been big league players, or they have played in the minors or managed in the minors for years. It isn't so difficult to figure out when to change pitchers. But the secret of managing is to give the players the credit that is due them, and to treat them like men. If they want to drink in the hotel bar, they should. That's their bar. I can go someplace else. If they want an extra hour before curfew, give it to them. If they want to stay home and spend the off day with their families, let them. If they act like men, they'll be treated like men. If they act like little boys, they'll be treated like little boys.

I have very few rules. Play hard for me, give

me everything you have when you're on that field. Don't take advantage of me. Don't embarrass me; if you do, I'm going to embarrass you right back.

What I try to do is wait until the next day before I say something to a player who has screwed up. Sometimes I forget and blurt it out right then and that's wrong. I know it's wrong and I try to make a point of apologizing for doing it. But I'm human and I have a short fuse sometimes.

There is a big difference between second-guessing and constructive criticism. I try not to reprimand a player for something he has done wrong without suggesting a solution or correction. That, to me, is constructive criticism, not second-guessing.

You have to know when to tell players they screwed up without hurting them. How do you know? I can't answer that. It's one of those things that have to come instinctively.

I have made my share of mistakes on that. Every manager makes mistakes. I never get mad at a player for making an error that's the result of overaggressiveness. The strategy part of managing came easy to me. I manage like I used to play. Aggressive. Force the other team to make mistakes. You can't be afraid to make a move. If you are, you'll lose the confidence of your players.

It was this style of play that gave birth to the term "BillyBall." A writer in Oakland came up with the term. It wasn't that I was doing anything different in Oakland from what I did everywhere else I managed. Everywhere I have played, for that matter. But this writer, Ralph Wiley, watched us win games with the double steal, with aggressive base running, with the suicide squeeze. He watched us gamble and take chances. He watched us try things that upset the opposition, forced them into making errors. He watched all this stuff, and it was successful, and one day he referred to this daring style of play as "BillyBall." Then it just caught on. Other writers started using it. They started using it on radio and TV. And the next thing you know, the Oakland club jumped on the slogan and began to use it in its promotional and advertising campaigns.

BillyBall is nothing more than just aggressive, old-fashioned baseball where you're not afraid to make a mistake. In other words, sticking your neck out to be aggressive. Smart aggressive. Not overhustle. BillyBall is forcing the opposition to make mental and physical mistakes. Going against the grain. Going after them all the time.

Take the extra base. Let the outfielders prove they can throw you out. Gamble. Force the other team to execute perfectly. Bunt when they're expecting a hit-and-run. Hit-and-run when they're expecting the bunt. Squeeze with your best power hitter. Hit away with your best bunter because the infield is drawn in. You'd be surprised, sometimes what you don't do is just as effective as what you do do. What I mean by that is that I have the reputation that I love the suicide squeeze. And I do. So what happens? Whenever there's a man on third with less than two outs, the other manager suspects the squeeze; he has his third baseman play in; I turn my hitter loose and he has a better chance of hitting one past the third baseman.

Catch them off guard. Get them looking for something, then hit them with something else. That's what baseball really is. The element of surprise. Always looking for an opportunity out there to create something. But get it quick. Right now. Not two innings from now. In other words, if the shortstop isn't holding the man on second, have him steal right then. Don't wait. If you wait, the shortstop might realize his mistake and correct it. So I'm looking for that opening all the time. Just give me a little room. I'm going to take advantage of it. What the hell. When you're a leader, you have to lead. That's when you stick your neck out. Leaders are not followers. They are innovators. They are gamblers. They're not afraid to take a chance, not afraid to fail. If they are, then they shouldn't be leaders.

That's why I have been successful as a manager, because I stick my neck out. Some managers manage not to lose instead of managing to win. They go by the book because they're afraid of being second-guessed by the fans, the press and especially the front office. You can't do that. You can't be timid. You have to have the courage of your convictions.

I know I'm not the easiest manager to play for or coach for. I'm tough. I'm demanding. I ride my coaches and players pretty hard. I get on them all the time and some of them don't like that. I'm constantly yelling at them. Remind. Remind. Remind. The same things over and over. I believe in repetition. I think that's the only way you can get to do things so they become second nature. It's the only way to avoid making mistakes.

In spring training, I'll have the players go over the same play hundreds of times—pickoff plays, pitcher covering first on a ground ball to the first baseman, pitchers backing up third base. Over and over, so they shouldn't forget to do it in a game. When a ball is hit on the ground to the right side, the pitcher should automatically break from the mound to cover first. When there's a runner on first and the hitter gets a base hit, the pitcher should automatically be on his way to back up third base.

We practice cutoffs from the outfield over and

over. Who should cut the ball off, when the ball should be cut off, where the outfielder should be throwing the ball. It's the little things that win ball games.

I believe in being thorough. I want my players to be smart and I want them to be aggressive. Physical errors are going to happen. They're part of the game because these are human beings playing out there. But I will not tolerate mental errors. I won't have a team that will beat themselves. That's where I set my priorities as a manager. I want my team to avoid making the mistakes that cause them to beat themselves. That's why I stay on my coaches and players as much as I do.

To be aggressive, a manager has to have good coaches. It's very important to me to have a good third base coach especially, someone who has to be thinking along with you. Not managing the game, but considering all the options and being ready for whatever I want to do. I have always given a lot of authority to my third base coach, and I have been fortunate to have had some very good ones.

Dick Howser was an excellent third base coach for me in New York and he became an outstanding manager. Gene Michael was a good third base coach. He went on to be the manager of the Chicago Cubs. Clete Boyer was my third base coach in Oakland and he developed into the best in the game because he learned to anticipate me and was always ready for anything. You can be sure I jumped his ass a lot in the beginning.

"Clete," I'd tell him, "don't manage the game, but consider all the possibilities and be ready for anything."

When I left Oakland, Clete stayed and he called all the signs for the A's. As a result, I found him the toughest to manage against because he knew all my moves. He had been a great fielding third baseman for

the Yankees after I left, the equal of Brooks Robinson
with the glove. In 1961, he practically beat the Cincinnati Reds in the World Series single-handedly with his
glove work. He's also a great teacher of young infielders. He's extremely patient with kids and he has a way
with young players that makes them want to learn.

"Clete," I'd say, "So-and-so did this; he's leaving too soon. He's tipping off the pitches."

"I'll get it, Billy," he'd say.

And the next day, it was done. Now I could be
sure that wherever I went, my back was covered.

A good third base coach can win you several
games a year. He has to be compatible with the manager. His thinking has to be the same as the manager's.
He has to know the speed of his runners, the strength
and accuracy of the throwing arms of every outfielder
in the league. He has to know when to gamble and
when not to gamble. He has to be able to think quickly
on his feet. Should I send this runner? Who's running?
Who's throwing the ball? Who's the catcher? Who's the
next batter? What's the score? How many are out? All
this knowledge he must have at his fingertips so that he
can make a snap judgment that could mean the difference between winning and losing a game.

Be in the ball game at all times. Make sure the
runner on second is getting a good lead. Yell at him.
Make him get off another step. Don't worry if he gets
mad at you. Make him think about tagging up on a long
fly. The third base coach has to do all that.

And he has to pass along the manager's signs.
That's not as easy as it seems. People are stealing signs
all the time. You have to be careful. And you have to be
alert.

For instance, when the other team is changing
pitchers, I'll give my third base coach a sign when ev-

erybody's attention is diverted. Clete knows enough to be looking at me. Other third base coaches might be talking with the umpire during the lull, talking with the third baseman, looking at some broad in the stands. Not Clete. He knows enough to be paying attention, looking at me in case I have a sign I want to give.

If the count goes to 3 and 0, I'll give my third base coach the steal sign, meaning: "If this guy gets on, I want him running on the first pitch or the second pitch." I won't wait until he gets the walk. I'll give the sign before the walk. So that after the walk, when the other team looks at me to try to pick up the steal sign, I'll be going through decoy signs to throw them off. My third base coach already has received the steal sign.

Just as important as the third base coach is my pitching coach. My pitching coach has to be a good teacher and a psychologist. I don't need a pitching coach once the game starts. Then, I can be my own pitching coach. I can tell when my pitcher is losing his stuff, when he's tiring. I make the pitching changes myself. I'm not going to pass the buck on those decisions and let somebody else do it.

What I want from a pitching coach is for him to gain the confidence of his pitchers. I don't care what you have heard about Art Fowler, he was an outstanding pitching coach for me and for one reason: He was my buffer with the pitchers. To me, Art was exactly what a pitching coach should be, a friend to the pitchers yet close with the manager.

Let me tell you about Arthur Fowler. I first ran across Art when I went to Denver to manage in 1968. I had heard of him before then. He was a mediocre journeyman pitcher for Cincinnati and the Los Angeles Angels in the 1950s and 1960s. His major league record was 54–51. When I caught up with him in 1968, Art was

forty-seven years old and he was pitching for the Denver Bears. That's right, I said *pitching* at the age of
forty-seven. He was in his twenty-fifth year as a pitcher.
He turned out to be my bullpen stopper that year, and
my unofficial pitching coach.

The following year, when I went to Minnesota
to manage, I took Art with me as my pitching coach.
And he has been my pitching coach everywhere I have
managed—Detroit, Texas, New York and Oakland.

After I was fired in Minnesota, Art went back
to Denver as player-coach in 1970. He was forty-nine
years old and he won 9 games and saved 15 and was
voted the Most Valuable Player in the American Association that season. But Art wouldn't accept the award.
He said he didn't need it at his age and he told them to
give it to a young player.

Art is from Spartanburg, South Carolina, and
he has this thick Southern drawl that sometimes makes
it difficult to understand him. Especially when he has
been drinking. And Art has been known to take a beer
or two. In fact, one year he was picked up three times
for driving while impaired, and when I called him to
ask him how he could get nailed on the same charge
three times, he said the third time he was driving his
lawn mower on the grass.

The thing that made Art such an effective
pitching coach for me was that the pitchers loved him.
He'd smooth-talk them in that sweet Southern drawl of
his and they'd do anything for him.

"Do you know why Billy chewed your ass
out?" he'd say. "Because you screwed up, that's why.
Admit it. Admit you screwed up."

Art would get on his pitchers to do their running and the pitchers would always complain about it.

"But, Art, I don't want to run twenty laps. Why

do I have to run? Did you run when you were pitching?"

"Nooo," Art would say in that drawl of his. "But Beeellly wants ya ta run. Thas wah yo' gonna run."

Then while they're running, they're throwing baseballs at Art and yelling at him and they're having fun doing it. It's not a grind because they love Art and they're running because Art told them to and they enjoy him.

Once, in Oakland, I sent Art to the mound to talk to Matt Keough because he was so wild he was walking the ballpark. So Art goes out, and I find out later this is how the conversation went.

Keough: "What is it, Art?"

Fowler: "Whatever it is, you got Beeellly madder'n hell. He's chewing me out. So whatever it is you're doin', you better change it because I'm gettin' hell back on the bench."

That's Arthur. He's beautiful. I love him.

A manager has to have good instincts. He has to know what the other manager is thinking. You're not just guessing at it, you actually have an instinct or an intuition about what the other guy is going to do.

So many times the other manager would go to the mound to talk to his pitcher, for instance, and I'd say to my players, "He's telling him, 'Billy's going to send the runner, so we're going to pitch out.'"

And they'd pitch out and I wouldn't be sending the runner because I knew he was going to pitch out. And I have said it on the bench before it happens and the players would say, "How did you know that?"

I don't know how I knew it. It's just instinct, or intuition.

As I have said before, a manager's biggest job is done before and after a game. He might have to kick ass or he might have to stroke a player who's going bad and needs a boost of confidence. Or he might have to talk to a player who hasn't been playing. I have had players who would get upset if you didn't say hello to them every day. You have to do that because even if he's the last player on your roster, you have to keep him motivated and involved, for there is going to come a time when you will need him to fill in for a day or two, or to pinch-hit, or pinch-run, and you want him to be ready to give you his best. You have to let even the twenty-fifth player know that he is an important part of the team.

I know I have a reputation for being quick on the draw. And I have had my problems with players. But they have been in the minority. To give you an example, during the 1977 season George Steinbrenner once accused me of trying to be too close with the players. He suggested I should be more aloof, but I couldn't do it.

If I have a problem with a player, I try not to let it carry over to the next day. It happened. It's forgotten. I also try never to let my personal feelings for a player, or the problem I have had with him, influence me when it comes to playing him. I know there are people who are going to read that and say, "Bullshit," but believe me, to the best of my ability, I have tried to hold to that code.

As a manager, I have always tried to protect my players. I may chew out a player, but I try never to chew him out in the newspapers if I can help it. With one exception. If the player does it first, then I'm going to come back at him. That's when I become a counterpuncher. Rip me in the papers and I'm likely to rip you right back. Embarrass me on the ball field, I'm likely to embarrass you.

I don't think there's ever a generation gap in baseball. I do think there's a terminology gap. You and the player may be saying different things, but you have the same objective. I think you have to really listen to today's kids and you have to change your thinking along with them. I am proud to say I have an excellent relationship with my son, Billy Joe. He's twenty-two, just about the age of many major league players, so I feel I can relate to these players because I can relate to my own son.

When you're managing, you should keep an open mind so that you can learn something new every year. Something happens out there on the ball field that you've never seen before. And when it does, you have to have an answer for the player who asks, "How do you defend against that play?" As a manager, you have to know how to do it. If I teach them how to defend against the bunt, then I have to teach them how to beat that same defense against the bunt.

A manager has to change every year. The game is changing constantly and you have to change right along with it. A manager cannot stay the same year after year. If he does, he becomes stagnant and predictable and that's when the game passes him by, the young managers pass him by, and he loses his effectiveness.

In the game of baseball, I don't think you can ever say to yourself, "Now I know it all." Because when you do, you stop improving. And when you stop improving, you become obsolete. Especially in a game like baseball. Just when you think you have seen it all, that's when something happens that you have never seen before.

11

When George Steinbrenner brought me back to manage the Yankees for the fourth time early in the 1985 season, one of the first things he did was call me into his office.

"Now, Billy," he said, "I don't want you to hurt my pitchers' arms. We have some kids here who are valuable to us. They're going to be good pitchers and I don't want you pitching them too many innings. Also, So-and-so can't go more than seven innings. And don't bring Righetti in too early. And another thing . . ."

I know what people say about me. I hear the rumors. I can read. I know what people think. They say I can't handle pitchers. I overwork them. I overpitch them. I hurt their arms. I don't care about their future, only about winning here and now for my own selfish reasons.

You know what I say to all of that?

Bullshit!

I know exactly how all that got started and I know how, and why, it's being repeated. It's passed along by owners and managers who have to justify firing me; by other baseball people who are jealous of my success; and by writers who don't like me and are always looking for some way to knock me.

It got started because four of my pitchers in Oakland came down with sore arms. And everybody said it was because I overworked them.

When I got to Oakland in 1980, I settled on a five-man starting rotation made up of Rick Langford, Matt Keough, Mike Norris, Steve McCatty and Brian Kingman. Langford had come over from the Pirates three years earlier in one of the shrewdest trades Charlie Finley ever made. He gave the Pirates Phil Garner, who was a good, hard-nosed second baseman, veteran infielder Tommy Helms and a pitcher named Chris Batton. Garner was the guy the Pirates wanted and he was a good player for them for several years. Helms was finished. He played one more season, then retired. Batton never pitched for the Pirates, or any other big league team, after he was traded.

In exchange, Finley got Tony Armas, who became one of the American League's top power hitters, Mitchell Page, who had 17 or more home runs three times for Oakland, pitchers Doc Medich, Dave Giusti and Doug Bair, who were used in other trades to other teams, and Langford, who, as I said, was in my five-man rotation in 1980. The other four were signed by Oakland as free agents.

Keough, another member of the starting rotation, was the son of Marty Keough, who was a journey-man outfielder-first baseman for eleven seasons with several major league teams.

In 1980, Langford, Norris and Keough finished 1–2–3 in the American League in complete games. And that was supposed to be the reason they all later came down with arm problems.

Bullshit!

What people forget is that in 1981 there was a players' strike that lasted about two months, and during that time the players were supposed to stay in shape on their own. Whether they did or didn't, I had no idea. Managers and coaches were not allowed to supervise any workouts, so I just had to assume these guys were adult enough, professional enough, dedicated enough and intelligent enough to take care of themselves and stay in shape without supervision. After all, it's their livelihoods.

So for two months, I wasn't there and my pitching coach, Art Fowler, wasn't there to see that my pitchers did their work, warmed up properly, did their running, wore a jacket when they were sweating, threw with the proper motion— all the things that managers and pitching coaches have to watch to baby their pitchers. And I'm convinced the sore arms that came later were the result of improper training during the strike, not overwork.

Ask any veteran pitcher and I guarantee you he will say the same thing; you can't hurt an arm by throwing too much. Inactivity is much more harmful. Veteran pitchers like Tommy John, Jim Kaat and Phil Niekro will tell you that they wanted to throw every day to keep their arm strong. Each will agree there's no such thing as overwork, and look at how long their careers lasted and how successful they were—over 850 wins, 2,400 games, 14,000 innings and 71 major league seasons among the three of them.

Those Oakland pitchers of mine were later interviewed by *Sports Illustrated* and each of them said it wasn't my fault that their arms blew out. They blamed it on a variety of things. Matt Keough, for instance, completely absolved me of any blame for his sore arm.

"Billy is not responsible for my sore arm," Keough said. "Billy was great. I hurt my arm when I slipped on a wet mound in Chicago."

Sure, we had a lot of complete games in Oakland in 1980 and 1981. One reason was that I didn't have a bullpen I could rely on, so I asked my starters to go longer because they were better pitchers tired than my relievers were fresh. That didn't mean I left them in if I thought they were struggling and so used up they were in danger of hurting themselves. Even if you want to believe I don't care about pitchers' arms, would you believe that I would leave a tired pitcher in there and risk blowing a ball game?

Another reason I let my starters go longer was that they were very effective that season; you don't take a pitcher out of a game when he's pitching well. The third and most important reason is that although these guys were pitching nine innings, they weren't making a lot of pitches. Langford, for example, was completing games with as few as seventy-four pitches, and as I've said over and over, it's not the number of innings a pitcher pitches that counts, it's the number of pitches he makes.

That's why it pissed me off when George called me in and warned me not to hurt his pitchers' arms.

"George," I said, "can I just tell you something about pitching?"

"What's that?"

"It's not the number of innings a pitcher pitches that counts, it's the number of pitches he throws. Let me explain. Here's a pitcher who throws seventy-five pitches in a nine-inning game. Here's another pitcher who throws a hundred and thirty-five pitches. They both pitch nine innings. Who's putting more wear and tear on his arm?

"I've been trying to tell you for years. This guy goes out and throws eighty pitches in nine innings. Another guy may throw a hundred and thirty-five pitches and not get out of the fifth inning. You'll look at innings pitched and decide the second guy is rested and the first guy is overworked. But I'll look at pitches thrown. Innings don't count. Pitches count."

Let's look at that 1980 pitching staff in Oakland. Not one of my pitchers pitched 300 innings that year. And the following year, because of the strike, we lost one third of the season and Langford led our staff in innings pitched with 195, which didn't even lead the league. How are you going to make a charge of overworking pitchers stick when none of them ever pitched 300 innings in one season and one third of the season was missing in another?

Back when I was playing, it was nothing unusual for pitchers to work more than 300 innings in a season. Teams were using a four-man rotation instead of a five and the use of relief pitchers was not as prevalent as it is now. Pitchers finished what they started. So all I was doing with my Oakland staff was reverting to the way the game was played thirty or forty years before.

Langford made 33 starts in 1980. Even a power pitcher like Bob Feller made anywhere from 35 to 42 starts in seven consecutive seasons in the 1940s and 1950s, with time out for military service.

Back in 1904, a guy named Jack Chesbro had 53 decisions for the Yankees, or the New York Highlanders, as they were called in those days. He started 51 games, completed 48, pitched four times in relief, worked 454.2 innings and had a record of 41 and 12.

The great Cy Young had five seasons in which he pitched more than 400 innings, and sixteen in which he pitched 300 innings or more. And he pitched for twenty-two seasons.

It is also important to point out that while I was in Oakland, not one of my pitchers came down with a sore arm. They all had their problems after I was gone. So why blame me?

People seem always to be singling out pitchers who pitched for me and came down with sore arms to prove their point that I am not a good handler of pitchers. How about the guys who pitched for me and never had an arm problem? Ron Guidry never had an arm problem. I had Catfish Hunter at the end of his career and he never had an arm problem. I had Jim Kaat when he was young and he pitched until he was forty-five and he never had an arm problem.

Let's look at my record with pitchers. I'm not afraid to match it up with any other manager's. Let's look at all the pitchers I had who were 20-game winners. Ron Guidry three times. Mickey Lolich twice. Joe Coleman twice. Jim Perry. Dave Boswell. Ferguson Jenkins. Mike Norris.

That's eleven 20-game winners in fourteen years of managing and I'm including 1981, the strike year, but I probably shouldn't. I'm also including some years when I didn't hang around for the full season for reasons that were not always of my choosing. Sparky Anderson once told me that with all those great Cincinnati teams in the era of the Big Red Machine, he only had one 20-game winner.

And I'm not including the 19-game winners, Ed Figueroa in New York, Jim Bibby in Texas and Joe Coleman in Detroit.

When I got to Detroit in 1971, Mickey Lolich had just come off the poorest year of his career. He won only 14 games in 1970 and lost 19, the most in the league. In 1971, he led the league with 25 wins and lost only 14. He won 22 in 1972 and was 16–15 for me in 1973.

Then I left. His records for the next few seasons were 16–21, 12–18, 8–13.

I knew Joe Coleman's dad, Joe Senior. Hit against him when he pitched for the Philadelphia Athletics. Junior had come to Detroit from Washington in a trade involving Denny McLain, the first trade the Tigers made after I became manager. For Washington in 1970, Coleman had won 8 games and lost 12. In six seasons, he had never won more than 12. In my three years in Detroit, he won 62 games—20, 19 and 23. In the three years after I left Detroit, he won 28 games—14, 10 and 4.

In ten seasons before I had him, Jim Perry never won 20 games. He won 20 for me in Minnesota in 1969, and, as proof that I didn't hurt him, he won 24 for Bill Rigney in 1970. He never won 20 again, but he pitched until 1975, finally retiring at the age of thirty-nine after he had pitched seventeen seasons and won 215 major league games.

In five seasons with the Minnesota Twins before I got there, Dave Boswell won a total of 44 games, an average of 9 wins a season, never more than 14 in any one season. In 1969, he won 20. He never won 20 games again.

Fergie Jenkins was an outstanding pitcher for nineteen major league seasons, a possible Hall of Famer. In his career, he won 284 major league games. Seven times he won 20 or more. But his highest victory total in any one season was the 25 he won for me with Texas in 1974. And I didn't ruin him, for he went on to pitch nine more years after that, but the most he ever won in a season after 1974 was 18.

Mike Norris had won 5 games the year before I got to Oakland, a total of 12 games in five seasons. He won 22 for me in 1980.

I had Ed Figueroa in New York. He came over from the California Angels in 1976. In two seasons with the Angels, he won 18 games. He won 19 for me in 1976 and 16 in 1977. In 1978, when I split the season as manager with Bob Lemon, Figgy won 20, the first native-born Puerto Rican to win 20 games.

Jim Bibby had won 10 games in two seasons when I got to Texas. He won 19 for me in 1974 and pitched in the big leagues for ten more seasons.

I am indebted to Leonard Koppett, one of the most knowledgeable sportswriters around. Koppy had worked in New York when I was playing with the Yankees and later he moved to the Bay Area and was there when I managed the Oakland club. Koppett loves to play with figures and one day recently he showed me something that makes the point better than I ever could. It has to do with my five starters in Oakland—Langford, McCatty, Keough, Norris and Kingman.

Remember that I managed in Oakland in 1980–81–82. Now let's take those pitchers one at a time.

Langford: In 1979 (the year before I got there), his earned run average was 4.27. In the three years I was there, his ERA was 3.26, 3.00 and 4.21. In the year after I left, his ERA was 12.15.

McCatty: In 1979, his ERA was 4.21. In my three years, it was 3.85, 2.32, 3.99. The three years after I left it was 3.99, 4.76, 5.57.

Keough: He went from 5.03 in 1979 to 2.92, 3.41 and 5.72 (my years) to 5.33.

Norris: In the three years before I arrived, his ERA was 4.79, 5.51, 4.81. In my three years, it was 2.54, 3.75, 4.76.

Kingman: He was 4.30 in 1979 and 4.48 in 1983, the year before I got there and the year after I left. In my three years, his ERA was 3.84, 3.96, 3.54.

Chart those numbers on a graph. You'll see the Martin years represented by the low on the curve. Not bad for a guy who isn't supposed to know pitching, who has picked up a reputation that he hurts pitchers. And before I forget, or mislead you, just a reminder that what I have just demonstrated about Billy Martin, manager, also goes for Art Fowler, pitching coach.

I haven't talked about Ron Guidry. I will now.

I have been a Ron Guidry man as long as I can remember. I'm the guy who made him a starter. When I got to the Yankees in 1975, Guidry was the subject of many debates among the Yankee brass. Everybody knew he had a great arm, but opinion was divided on him. Some thought he would never make it and wanted to trade him. Others wanted to keep him. Some wanted to pitch him out of the bullpen. Some thought he should be a starter. I had no role in any of this, but in 1977 he was in my starting rotation. George kept telling me he couldn't start, that he couldn't pitch more than six innings. Later, I was supposed to have burned out his arm. That was almost ten years ago. One day early in the season, I got Gator over the hump. He was in the ninth inning for the first time and he had a four- or five-run lead.

All of a sudden, I'm a son of a bitch, before I knew it, we had a one-run lead and the bases were loaded. The situation called for a relief pitcher, but I made up my mind I wasn't going to bring in a relief pitcher. Sometimes a pitcher will use the bullpen as a crutch. You'll see some starters take a peek over their shoulder to see who's warming up. They're looking to bail out of there, give somebody else the ball and the mess they've created. I was going to prove to Guidry, and everybody else, that he could go nine innings.

I knew I was risking blowing a ball game. But there are times a manager has to take a gamble like that. You risk losing this game to discover a pitcher who is going to help you down the line, for the rest of the season.

That's what I was doing with Brian Fisher in September 1985 when I left him in to take a beating and wound up blowing a ball game. I got a lot of criticism for that, but I had a reason for what I did.

We had just lost those three straight to Toronto and were in the middle of that horrendous eight-game losing streak. We were playing the Cleveland Indians in Yankee Stadium and we had a lead, but the Indians rallied to go ahead against Fisher. I just left Brian in there to take a lumping and the writers really got on me for that one.

But Fisher was throwing the ball good and, at one point, I went to the mound with every intention of taking him out of there.

There's no set thing you say when you go out to the mound to talk to the pitcher. It depends on the situation, the score, the pitcher. Mostly, it depends on your reason for being out there.

Sometimes it's to remind the pitcher how you want him to pitch to a certain hitter. Sometimes it's just to give him a rest. Sometimes it's to stall so your relief pitcher can get warmed up. Sometimes it's to chew ass. Sometimes to offer encouragement. Sometimes you have a mission, you're bringing in a new pitcher.

It's absolutely taboo for a manager to go out there and ask the pitcher if he wants to come out if you have already made up your mind before you get out there. I will not let a pitcher talk me out of taking him out. I will let him talk me out of leaving him in.

What I mean is that if I am certain he should come out, I won't even discuss it with him, I'll just make the move. If I am uncertain, I'll let him tell me. A veteran pitcher I might just ask, point-blank, "Are you tired?" Most of them will level with you.

Another pitcher I might just question if I have any doubts. If he doesn't seem too confident, I will take him out.

You can't ask the catcher how he thinks the pitcher is throwing. At least, you can't ask him in front of the pitcher. He might lie to spare the pitcher's feelings. And 95 times out of 100, if you ask the pitcher if he's tired, he's going to say no because he wants to stay in there.

When I went out to see Brian Fisher, I know what I wanted to hear. I wanted him to stay in, but I wanted him to tell me. If he was wishy-washy about it, I would have yanked him. Brian was anything but wishy-washy.

"You're throwing the ball good, aren't you?" I said, to kind of blow smoke his way, boost his confidence. I was stroking him.

"Yeah," he said. "They're just hitting everything I'm throwing up there."

Then I asked him the important question, thinking I already knew what the answer would be.

"You want to come out?"

"Oh, please, Billy," he said. "Let me stay in."

It was exactly what I expected to hear. And exactly what I wanted to hear.

"O.K.," I said.

I left him in, but I had a method to my madness that the writers would not understand.

For one thing, I wanted to save my bullpen. For another, I wanted Fisher to know that every once in a while a pitcher has to take a lumping to help make him a better competitor. He's getting hit and it's embarrassing, but the easy thing to do is get him out of there. By leaving him in, it toughens him. Fisher was a rookie and I was going to need him later in the season. By leaving him in there, I'm showing him that I have confidence in him. And that might be important later.

I could have taken him out and I might have lost him. He might have lost his confidence and been useless to me for the rest of the season. He had to take this lumping. Every once in a while, every pitcher has to tough it out for the good of the team. By leaving him in there, I saved my pitching staff for the next three days instead of using them up.

Another thing, I don't like to bring in my ace relief pitcher in a losing cause. I get criticized a lot for that.

"Why didn't you bring in Righetti?"

We're three runs down, that's why. This game is lost as far as I'm concerned. Now, if the score is tied or we're one run down, I might bring in my best relief pitcher.

Anyway, I left Fisher in to take his lumps and we lost the game, but I didn't lose Brian Fisher. He pitched very well for me the rest of the season, but he might not have if I had taken him out that day against Cleveland.

And that's exactly what I was doing with Guidry that day in 1977. If I had taken him out in the ninth, he'd never know if he could go nine. He'd think I had no confidence in him and he'd lose confidence in himself. I had to get him over the hump.

So I went to the mound and I said to him, "You think you're coming out? No way. We're going to prove once and for all that you can go nine innings."

He struck out the next hitter and from that day on he was over the hump.

Let's examine the record of Ron Guidry. Prior to 1977, he hadn't won a game in the major leagues. He was up and down between New York and Syracuse several times until he came up to stay in 1977, which was my second full season as manager of the Yankees. Here's Guidry's record from the time he became a mainstay of the Yankees pitching staff:

Year	W–L	Starts	Complete Games	Innings	ERA	K	Manager
1977	16–7	25	9	211	2.82	176	Martin
1978	25–3	35	16	274	1.74	248	Martin (94 games) Lemon (68 games)
1979	18–8	30	15	236	2.78	201	Lemon (64 games) Martin (96 games)
1980	17–10	29	5	220	3.56	166	Howser
1981	11–5	21	0	127	2.76	104	Michael, Lemon
1982	14–8	33	6	222	3.81	162	Lemon, Michael, King
1983	21–9	31	21	250.1	3.42	156	Martin
1984	10–11	28	5	195.2	4.51	127	Berra
1985	22–6	33	11	259	3.27	143	Berra (16 games) Martin (145 games)
1986	9–12	30	5	192.1	3.98	140	Piniella

I had Guidry in 1977, for the first half of the 1978 season, for the second half of the 1979 season, for the entire 1983 season and for all but sixteen games in the 1985 season. Ron has had three seasons in which he won 20 games or more—in 1978 (when I had him for the first half), in 1983 (I was there all season) and in 1985 (I was there most of the season).

He had two losing seasons, in 1984 and again in 1986. I know, people are going to say that I pitched him too much in 1983, which is why he didn't win in 1984. Then how come he won in 1985? And how come he lost in 1986?

In the years I had him for the entire season, he made 25 starts in 1977, 31 in 1983, 33 in 1985. He pitched 211 innings in 1977, 250 in 1983, 259 in 1985. In 1978 and 1979, I split the season as manager with Bob Lemon, so Lem has to take at least half the blame (or credit) for Guidry's numbers. In 1978, he started 35 games and pitched 274 innings. In 1979, he had 30 starts and only 236 innings. I hardly think that's over-working a pitcher. Look at it this way. In 1985, Dwight Gooden of the New York Mets pitched more innings than Ron Guidry pitched in any of his nine seasons. And Gooden was in only his second major league season. But I never heard anybody say Davey Johnson overworked Gooden.

The bottom line is this. Guidry has started almost 300 games in his major league career, he has pitched more than 2,000 innings and he never has had any serious arm trouble.

What matters is the record: my performance and the performance of the pitchers who have pitched for me. I think you will have to admit, from what you have just seen, that the record stacks up very well in my defense.

12

I'm sure my detractors are saying, "What does Billy Martin know about pitching? The only thing he knows about pitching is that he couldn't hit it."

Not true. Check my lifetime batting average. For eleven seasons, over 1,000 games, it was .257. Maybe that wasn't good enough to get me elected to the Hall of Fame, but these days it would be good enough to get me a seven-figure contract. Check my lifetime batting average in the World Series. In 28 games, covering 99 at bats, it was .333 with five home runs and 19 RBIs. I always was a better player in big games, I guess I just needed that extra motivation to do my best. Some guys are like that, just like some actors.

They will perform better in front of a large audience than they do in front of a half-empty house.

That was me in the World Series. Project my Series stats over a full season, about 600 at bats, and it comes to 30 home runs and 114 RBIs. That's Hall of Fame material and that alone should qualify me as an expert on the subject of pitching. I'm not claiming that. What I am saying is, as my old buddy Yogi once said, "You observe a lot by watching." And I have been watching major league pitching for almost forty years now. I had to learn something.

I learned enough to win more than 1,200 games as a manager and have a winning percentage just a shade under 55 percent. I also learned enough to know how to pitch certain hitters. You don't have to be a pitcher to know about pitching. I'm not a mechanic, but I know how to drive a car. I also know that you don't have to be too smart to know that if a hitter can't hit a curveball, you throw him curveballs.

If there's one thing that burns my ass as a manager, it's when pitchers (and catchers) deliberately disobey my instructions because they try to think out there. I can give you hundreds of examples of what I mean. I'll give you one.

I'm managing the Texas Rangers and we're playing the Baltimore Orioles. My buddy Earl Weaver again. I have Jim Sundberg catching and we have a one-run lead in the ninth inning and the Orioles have a runner on second base with two outs. One more out and we win. I go to the mound and Sundberg joins me there.

"I'm going to make a switch," I say. "I'm going to bring in the left-hander [Mike Kekich] and I know Weaver is going to send up Andy Etchebarren to pinch-hit. Now, Etchebarren hasn't played in three weeks. He just came off the disabled list and his timing is off."

I have Sundberg right there and I signal to the umpire that I want the left-hander, Kekich, and he comes to the mound.

"I want you to throw him nothing but curve-balls," I tell him. "I don't care if you walk him. That's O.K. Then I can bring in a right-hander when Weaver makes his move. O.K., got it? Nothing but curveballs. Etchebarren can't hit a curveball with a paddle. Remember, nothing but curveballs. I don't care if you walk him. Got it?"

"Got it, Billy," Sundberg and Kekich both say.

I couldn't be clearer than that, could I? I even said it several times to make sure there was no mistake.

First pitch. Curveball. Strike one.

Second pitch. Curveball. In the dirt. Etchebarren swings and misses. Strike two.

Next pitch. Fastball. Triple.

I'll be a son of a bitch. What did I just say no more than five minutes before? Now I walk to the mound, madder than hell.

"What the f—— is going on here?"

"We were going to waste the fastball, then come back with the curve," says Kekich.

"You wasted it all right," I said.

The next day I sent Kekich back to the minor leagues.

Sundberg: "He shook me off, Billy."

"Awwww. He shook you off. Poor Sundberg. What's the matter, you couldn't walk out there sixty feet and tell him, 'Billy wants you to throw a curve-ball'?"

I believe in making the hitter prove he can hit a certain pitch. If you know he can't hit that pitch, keep throwing it to him until he proves to you he can hit it. I realize that it's necessary to change your pitching pattern from time to time and throw him something else. You give most hitters a steady diet of one pitch and sooner or later they catch on to what you're doing and they can sit on that pitch. Most major league hitters can hit a pitch if they know it's coming. Or they will improve at hitting a certain pitch if they see enough of them.

So you don't give a hitter a steady diet of one pitch. But you can pick your spots. You might be pitching a certain hitter one way, but say you have a four- or five-run lead. Then you might change your pattern and throw him the pitch you know he can hit, just to show it to him; to get him thinking the next time he bats; to cross him up. But if the game is on the line, why throw him the pitch you know he can hit? Don't give the hitter so much credit. Make him prove to you he can hit the other pitch.

Look at what happened to Tommy Lasorda in the final game of the 1985 National League Championship Series against the St. Louis Cardinals.

Jack Clark beat Tommy's Dodgers a game, and a pennant, by hitting a fastball off Tom Niedenfuer for a game-winning three-run homer in the ninth inning with first base open. Everybody knows Clark is a home run hitter—the only legitimate home run threat the Cardinals had. And everybody in baseball knows he's a dead fastball hitter.

Whether or not Lasorda should have walked Clark intentionally is another matter, but I can understand Lasorda not wanting to. I'm sure Tommy had his reasons. Maybe he didn't want to load the bases and put more pressure on his pitcher. But pitching to Clark in that situation, with first base open, there is no way he should have seen a pitch he could drive out of the ballpark. And there's no way he should have seen a fastball. What Lasorda should have done was go out and remind Niedenfuer to throw Clark nothing but breaking balls and not to worry if he walked him.

To his credit, Lasorda never second-guessed his pitcher. At least not publicly. But I have to believe that Tommy wanted nothing but breaking balls and his pitcher disobeyed. I guess we'll never know, because, for a change, Tommy's not talking.

One player who comes to mind is Aurelio Rodriguez. "Chi Chi," they called him. He played for me at Detroit in 1971–72–73. He was an outstanding third baseman with a howitzer for an arm and one of the most pleasant guys to be around. Chi Chi was always smiling, never complaining. He wasn't a very good hitter, only a .237 lifetime batter, unless he got his pitch. Chi Chi could murder a fastball. But he couldn't hit a curveball with a tennis racquet.

Let me explain something here. When I say a major league hitter can't hit a curveball or he can't hit a fastball, that is, of course, an oversimplification. These are major leaguers and even a guy who you can get out with curveballs will hit some curveballs. Hangers or lazy curveballs, or curveballs in bad locations. What I mean, then, is that these guys are vulnerable to curveballs if they are at least halfway decent pitches in good locations.

One time, I was managing the Oakland club and Chi Chi was playing for the Yankees and I instructed my pitcher to throw him nothing but curveballs in a critical situation. So what happens?

Curveball. Strike one.
Curveball. Strike two.
Fastball. Double.

Why?

"Gee, Billy, we can't keep throwing him curveballs."

"Why not? He can't hit them."

Or: "We were just going to show him the fastball, to set him up, then come back with the curveball."

You get beat more with setup pitches than with any other pitch in baseball.

Let me repeat that.

YOU GET BEAT MORE WITH SETUP PITCHES THAN WITH ANY OTHER PITCH IN BASEBALL.

That's why I get in so many arguments with catchers. I'm not trying to second-guess them. I'm trying to get them to think back there.

When you see a guy miss a pitch by a wide margin and not even have a good swing at the pitch and then the catcher doesn't come back with the same pitch, you wonder why. Maybe it's because the catcher can't see how far out in front the hitter was because of the catcher's vantage point. Well, I can see it from the bench. So if the catcher can't see it and I can, why won't he listen to me? It can't be because the catcher is dumb, can it?

I've said to Butch Wynegar a lot of times, "Why did you go away from the curveball and to the fastball?"

And he'll say, "I was going to come back with the curveball."

Was? When was he going to do it? After the game was over?

"Butch," I'll say, "when a guy can't hit a breaking ball and he shows you time and time again that he can't hit a breaking ball, why would you switch? Go

right after him with the breaking ball until he proves he
can hit it."

No, Butch wanted to do it the smart way. He
wanted to set up hitters.

"No, Butch," I'd say. "Do it my way. Do it the
dumb way and let's win."

Catchers always think you're second-guessing
them when you ask them why they did such and such.
But it's not second-guessing. I told them what to do
before the game started. So that's not second-guessing;
it's first-guessing.

"Why did you do this instead of what I told you
to do?"

"I forgot, Billy."

He forgot!

Can you believe it? He forgot. A catcher can't
forget. What else does he have to do for three hours out
there? Why is it that I can remember how to pitch
every batter in their lineup, every batter in the league,
how to play every hitter, and they can't?

That's why we go over scouting reports every
day. The pitching coach sits with the catcher and the
pitcher and goes over how we want to pitch every
hitter. The other coaches get together with the infielders and outfielders and go over how we are going to
play every hitter. Every day.

I can't keep going out to the mound every
time to remind the pitcher and the catcher how we
want to pitch a certain hitter. For one reason, there's a
rule that you can visit the mound only twice in an
inning, and the second time the pitcher must come out.
So I have to save those visits for crucial situations, or to
change a pitcher. For another reason, even if you could
go out to the mound on every hitter, you wouldn't want
to keep doing it because it breaks a pitcher's concentra-

tion and his momentum. That's why we have meetings before every game.

How come I have to yell at an infielder every time a certain batter comes up and tell him to move to his left or his right? Why can't he do his homework and know he should move before I tell him?

As soon as the batter comes to the plate, my infielder should be moving over automatically. He should know the hitter's tendency and how we plan to pitch him and he should play accordingly.

Why should I have to say to my coach, "Move him over again"?

Or: "There's two strikes on the hitter, tell the third baseman he can move back now, he doesn't have to worry about the bunt."

Why does a manager have to constantly do these things?

I'll tell you why. Because today's player is not in the game, that's why. He's thinking about other things. He's thinking about his contract, or his investments, or his family, or his last at bat. Or his next at bat. And that's the basic difference between today's player and the player of yesterday.

You hear a lot of discussion these days about the differences between the modern baseball player and the player of yesteryear. I'd like to get my two cents in on this discussion and tell you what I think are the major differences between today's ballplayer and the player of, say, thirty years ago. I don't know about the players of fifty or sixty years ago because I didn't see them. I can talk to you only from firsthand experience and, in my experience, the modern ballplayer is just as good as the old-time player. Better in some cases. He's just as good physically, that is.

Generally speaking, the modern player is bigger, stronger, faster and smarter than his predecessor. That stands to reason because human beings are bigger, stronger, faster and smarter. That's proved every day in other sports—the pole vaulter who easily goes over seventeen feet, the sprinter, the swimmer. If it's true in those other sports, there is no reason why it shouldn't be true in baseball.

Today's pitchers generally throw harder. In my day, they weren't timing the speed of pitches with radar guns, but when you heard about an Atley Donald or a Bob Feller throwing 95 miles an hour, it was the exception, not the rule. Today, every team has one or two pitchers who throw in the 90s consistently. Every team has a relief pitcher, or two, who can come in and throw smoke for an inning or two.

Today's player has better equipment, a better diet, better coaching. I still have the glove I used when I played second base for the Yankees, and occasionally I would take it out during batting practice and field ground balls. The players would look at it in disbelief. The glove is not much bigger than my hand. It's stiff and it has hardly any webbing. It's a relic. Today's gloves are like baskets. They're very supple and have huge webbing. You look at today's gloves and you wonder how a player can miss a ball. You look at mine and you wonder how we were able to catch with it.

Human beings today are much more diet-conscious than human beings of forty years ago. They know which are the proper foods to eat, and that goes for athletes, too. Take Wade Boggs, the great hitter for the Boston Red Sox. He'll eat nothing but chicken. Seven days a week, all he eats is chicken. He will not eat red meat. And doctors and dietitians will certainly tell you that chicken is better for you than red meat. Me, I love red meat.

Today's athlete also knows more about physical fitness, more about the human body. He'll stay in shape all year round by working out in the off-season. He'll use weights. He'll get into aerobics and Nautilus equipment in the off-season, things we never even heard of in my day. As a result, the baseball player of today comes to spring training in shape and ready to play. In my day, most players did nothing but lounge around all winter and they would come to camp overweight, so they would have to spend a good part of spring training getting in shape.

With all these advances, it stands to reason today's player is going to be better.

There are exceptions, of course. There always are. There are some players who would be stars in any era; some players who would adapt and adjust if they were around today. Babe Ruth never hit a slider, but I have no doubt he would be able to hit it. Just imagine how much greater Joe DiMaggio would have been if he used the kind of glove today's center fielders use. Don't try to tell me Mickey Mantle wasn't as strong or as fast as any player playing today. Think what Mick might have done if he had the advantage of modern medicine and training techniques to avoid all his injuries, or to bounce back much sooner after he was injured.

To me, the biggest difference between today's player and the old-time player is dollars. Today's players don't care about letters across their chest the way they did in my day. Here's Carlton Fisk. He had a good year with Boston. He's been with them for ten years. But he says, "Screw Boston, I'm going to Chicago because that's where the dollars are." There isn't that "Rah-rah, I'm a Yankee" or "Rah-rah, I'm a Red Sox" like it used to be. That's the difference.

There's not the togetherness there was when I

played, when we traveled together on trains. Or you get to a town and you all go off together or in large groups. Now, when the players get to a town, most of them have rental cars. They're not rooming two in a room anymore where you can talk baseball with your roommate. Now they live alone and a lot of them go out alone. There's no sitting in the lobby talking baseball because television keeps guys in their rooms. Everybody is so spread apart the only time they're together is when they are at the ballpark.

Some guys even have their families join them on the road. Look, I'm not against families, but let's face it, when the wife and kids are around, there are likely to be little problems and distractions that take your mind off baseball. It's your livelihood. Does the banker take his wife to the bank? Does the college professor take his kids into the classroom? Does the computer programmer have his family at his side? No.

Baseball isn't the number one thing to the modern player. It's his outside business that comes first or his investments or his real estate or his pension or his family. Then baseball. When I played, we actually put baseball ahead of our families. I'm not saying that's right, I'm just saying that's how it was.

The ability is there with today's player. The modern ballplayer is as good as or better than the old-timer. They have physical ability. But not all players have the mental ability for the game like the old-time player because some of them are not working as hard, because they don't spend as much time in the minor leagues learning their trade.

You get an owner who has a certain type of player for a certain amount of years and if you bench that player, he calls his agent, his agent calls the owner, the owner calls the manager and says, "What are you doing with this guy?"

What is the owner worried about? He's got the guy signed for five years. No, he doesn't want to hurt the player's feelings. More important, he doesn't want to hurt the agent's feelings and that has always bugged me. Why doesn't he want to hurt the agent's feelings? Because that agent might have another client who will be available the following year and the owner might have to be dealing with that agent the next year, or the year after. That's stupid.

Agents are hurting the game. So are long-term contracts. Players look at a manager and say, "Fine, Skip, say what you want, bench me if you want. I'm going to be here for five years, but you don't know where you'll be five years from now."

The player has the upper hand on the manager. He usually has a longer contract, he definitely makes more money and he can threaten to leave if he doesn't like the manager, so he even has the ability to dictate club policy. I have known some players who have gotten managers fired because the players couldn't get along with the managers. It used to be the other way around. Can you imagine a player in a power struggle with Joe McCarthy or Casey Stengel or Miller Huggins or John McGraw? Who do you think would win, the player or the manager?

Long-term contracts have removed the incentive from most modern players. In the old days, you used to get paid on the basis of what you did the previous year. Have a good year, you'll get a raise. Have a bad year, you might have to take a salary cut. When is the last time you heard about a player taking a salary cut?

In 1956, Mickey Mantle won the triple crown.

He batted .353, hit 52 homers, drove in 130 runs. He got a raise. And the next year he batted .365, had 34 homers and 94 RBIs and George Weiss, our general manager, wanted to cut him because he didn't have as good a year as he did the previous one. Mick eventually signed for the same salary.

What would Mickey Mantle and Joe DiMaggio be worth in today's baseball economy? Mick could get $3 million a year. I like what Joe D. said when someone asked him what he thought he would be worth in today's market.

"I'd just walk into the owner's office," said DiMag, "shake his hand and say, 'Hiya, partner.' "

Nowadays, with the long-term contracts, it doesn't matter if you have a good year or not. You have no incentive to have a good year because you are already signed for the following year, or two, or three. And that's bad. So you'll get the same salary next year whether you hit .350 or .250 this year, so where's the incentive to do better?

Another incentive in my day was the World Series share. I told you that in my first season my salary was $7,500 and my Series share was $6,400. So I made almost as much for a week's work as I did for six months' work. Naturally, you're going to try hard to get into the World Series because you need the money. Today, that incentive is gone. Sure, World Series shares are up as high as $80,000. But what's $80,000 to a player making $1 million a year?

Have you noticed, too, that players always play hard when they are in the final year of their contract?

Oh, there are exceptions. There always will be exceptions. There are players who have pride in their performance and have a good work ethic and who just simply want to win. These players are going to play hard no matter how much money they make or how long their contract. Dave Winfield is one guy who will always play hard, even though he has a ten-year contract. I didn't say he will always produce and have a great year, but he'll always play hard, run hard, dive for a ball, break up a double play, bust his ass. Don Mattingly is another. He'll always play hard. These guys have pride, they want to win. Others, no.

Casey Stengel would have a tough time managing today because of the agents and the way ownership has set up ball clubs. Casey wouldn't have the strength today that he had back when he was the sole power on the team. He didn't care if Gene Woodling hated his guts or Hank Bauer hated his guts. The hell with them. They're going to play the way he wanted them to play and that's the way the manager should have it.

Stengel played Bauer in right field against left-handed pitchers and Woodling in right field against right-handed pitchers and they both bitched about not playing every day, but what could they do? There were no agents in those days and they couldn't become free agents. They had to do what Casey said and like it. So they bitched, but they both hit .300, or close to it, almost every year and we won five straight world championships and Bauer and Woodling both went to the bank every year with their World Series checks just like the rest of us.

You're not going to see teams win five straight world championships any more unless you have a very strong organization. The only way to do it is to sign a Dave Winfield for ten years, and sign a Rickey Henderson for five years, and sign a Don Mattingly for five years. Now you have three key players all signed for at least five years. Then you have to work around those three positions. You have to do it cleverly. You have to get the type of young players you need for your short-stop of the future, your third baseman of the future. And you have to take a chance for a year or two that you won't win while you're molding your young players, helping them improve.

In the old days, you had large farm systems. Every team would have anywhere from twelve to twenty farm teams and some players would spend years in the minor leagues learning their craft before they came up to the majors. Joe DiMaggio played three years in the Pacific Coast League before they thought he was ready for the major leagues. But when he came up, he was ready. Other, lesser players would move up the ladder, Class D, Class C, Class B, Class A, seven years learning their trade. Today, if they're not in the big leagues after a year or two in the minors, they quit and try something else.

There used to be such great instruction in the minor leagues. Players would learn to do things the Yankee way or the Dodger way or the Cardinal way. They would learn it in the lowest minor league, all the way up to the majors, the same system.

The problem today is twofold. Players don't want to spend too much time in the minors, and owners aren't patient enough to suffer those two or three years without winning. They want instant success and they want it year after year and that's where you run into problems. That's when you sign these free agents from other clubs with huge salaries and you give them long-term contracts.

I don't give a damn what you say, you take a guy from another organization and he doesn't always fit in. He has different techniques, different habits, different coaching and instruction. It's important to have a certain chemistry on a baseball team, to have players who have played together for a few years and who know each other intimately, on the field and off.

You have to mold players. You have to get them to think your way, to do things your way. That's why it's so much easier to manage a bunch of kids. They haven't developed bad habits and they haven't become cliquish. That's why I was successful in Oakland. I had a bunch of kids and I was able to teach them to play the game my way. They were young and they were hungry to win, so they were eager to listen and learn.

Long-term contracts are often harmful. I'm not saying it's true with all players, but it is with many of them. They lose their incentive, their motivation, if they have a long-term contract. Subconsciously, they just don't seem to try as hard.

If a guy is a fringe player and it's time to sign him to a new contract, I'd like to see baseball just let him go. Bring in somebody else, somebody who won't cost as much money and who is hungrier, who is not set in his ways with all those bad habits. I'm not talking about a Don Mattingly or a Dave Winfield or a Rickey Henderson. Keep them. But get rid of the fringe players, just keep turning them over. That will stop all that nonsense of threatening the manager and the owner.

I believe in the old Army saying: "Every man can be replaced." Replace these malcontents and, believe me, somebody else will come along who will be just as good.

But the owners won't do it because they're afraid of the agents, so they'll extend the contracts of these malcontents, or renegotiate their contracts. And that's why you have the situation that exists today, the modern-day ballplayer who does nothing but bitch and cause problems.

One of my biggest disappointments with the Yankees in the 1985 season was when Don Baylor went up to the front office and asked to be traded because he didn't like the way I was using him. I was platooning him, using him as my designated hitter only against left-handed pitchers. Baylor is a very proud man and he felt he should have been playing every day, against all pitchers. I can respect that and I can appreciate his feelings. What I didn't appreciate was him going to the front office and asking to be traded in September. In the middle of a pennant race. Didn't he realize that was going to be an unnecessary distraction? Couldn't he understand that such a thing might undermine the common good of the team? Couldn't he wait until the season was over?

I have always respected and admired Don Baylor as a man and as a ballplayer. When he was playing for the California Angels, he was having problems with the team's president, Buzzie Bavasi. The two of them were going at each other in the papers almost every day. One night, before a game, I went on the field while the Angels were taking batting practice and I got Baylor off on the side alone.

"Don," I said. "You have a great future ahead of you. Don't get into any pissing contest in the papers with these guys. It won't do you any good and it could do you a lot of harm."

"Thanks, Billy," he said. "I really appreciate your advice."

I was just trying to help him because he and Bavasi were at it and you can't win against the front office. He stopped saying things in the paper and he wound up having an outstanding season.

Does Baylor forget this? Is his memory so short?

I'd have loved to have Baylor in there every day hitting. But when he goes up there and strikes out four times, doesn't get a hit in six days, I can't play him. We're in Yankee Stadium and I have left-handed hitters who can reach the seats and they're sitting on the bench because Baylor is playing and striking out. It isn't me and Baylor. It's what I think is best for the team. Does a team player go to the front office and ask to be traded with his team in a pennant race? Does a team player insist on playing every day at the expense of his teammates? What about the other players on the team?

Do I make mistakes? Sure I do. But I'm only doing what I think is best for the team, not what's best for Don Baylor or Billy Martin.

You can't get that across to these guys. Take a player out of one game and "Oh, you're not going to play me, then trade me." Bullshit. You know what these guys forget? I sat on the bench for two years when I first came up at the age of twenty after playing 187 games in the Pacific Coast League. You think I wasn't frustrated and pissed off? I was just happy to be with the Yankees. That's the difference. I was happy to be with the club. I could hardly wait for Yogi to make the last out so I could grab the mitt and run out there and warm up the pitcher while Yogi was putting on his shin guards and chest protector. That's the only time people would get a chance to see me. I got 36 at bats my first year and 58 at bats my second year.

You would sit there hoping you would get a chance to get in even if it was only as a pinch runner. Jackie Jensen beat me to it in the 1950 World Series. Casey needed a runner and Jensen got out there before I could.

You would just sit and wait for the opportunity to be out there. On the road, you would get three

swings in batting practice. Not three good pitches to hit
—three swings. That's the difference. The players of
today are too much "I" and not enough "we."

Still, as a manager you find yourself going out
of your way for them. I once played five guys on the last
day of the 1983 season with the Yankees because they
had bonus clauses and incentives based on number of
appearances. I sent Ron Guidry to the mound, then
moved him to center field because he had been pester-
ing me all year about playing the outfield and bragging
about what a good outfielder he was. I brought in
Tommy John to pitch because he needed one more
inning to get a $20,000 bonus. I must have cost George
about $300,000 that day.

I think some of the players appreciated what I
was doing, but a lot of them don't appreciate what you
do for them. They don't appreciate that you're fighting
for them behind their backs. Some of them don't even
know that you are.

Most players don't get to appreciate what you
have done for them until they're coming to the end of
the line or have retired. Then they realize. "Hey, that
man really did a good job for me. Maybe I didn't like all
the things he did, but he really helped me."

Just like I did with Casey Stengel.

With as much money as today's players are
making, they're always bitching and they're always unhappy. I can't believe it. How can you be unhappy
making $1 million a year for playing a game you love?

They'll be cheap in the clubhouse when it
comes to tipping the clubhouse man. You can't believe
how cheap they are, some of them. And they'll come in
after a game with their dirty hands and go right to the
food table. They can't wait to get to that damn food.
Even after losing the toughest game in the world, the

first thing they do is go right to the food table. And your coaches are right there along with them. That kills me. My stomach is in such knots after a tough loss that I couldn't even get any food down. I'd probably throw it right up if I did. But these guys are eating like the Russians are marching down Broadway. They really care!

Bullshit.

Then, boom, they're showered and they're gone, and you're sitting there saying, "What am I knocking myself out for? These guys don't even care. They don't care whether they win or lose."

All they care about is themselves.

"Play me. If you don't play me, I want my ball and bat and I want to go to another club. I don't want to play here anymore."

Nowadays, they all want to be traded if they think they're not being treated right, if the owner and the general manager are not revolving the entire team around them. I wish baseball would just release them. Nobody sign the SOBs. You don't want to play here? You don't like it here? Released. Go home. Go to work. You get no more salary, no more having your contract renegotiated, no more calling your agent or the Players' Association for every little thing.

I think the Commissioner should say he doesn't want to ever again hear any player saying he doesn't want to play for a particular team. If he does, he's automatically released. No money. That will stop all the bullshit.

These were two of the proudest days of my life. Left, the trophy presentation in our locker room the day the New York Yankees won the world championship in 1977. Below, Billy Martin Day at Yankee Stadium, August 10, 1986. They retired my No. 1 and the plaque next to me was erected in center field. Those are my sisters standing behind my mom in her wheelchair. Mom is wearing the pinstriped dress she had made especially for the occasion.

Don't you love those tight-fitting tapered uniforms we wore in my playing days? Here are some of my other memories:

Sluggo Martin crosses the plate after a home run in the 1952 World Series.

I would have knocked Dodger catcher Roy Campanella on *his* fanny if he wasn't wearing all that equipment.

I wasn't being a smart guy when I told our coach Frank Crosetti that I knew how to make the double play. I'm demonstrating it here (upper right) after getting the Dodgers' Gil Hodges at second.

Nobody was going after Jackie Robinson's pop fly in the 1952 World Series (right), so I took charge.

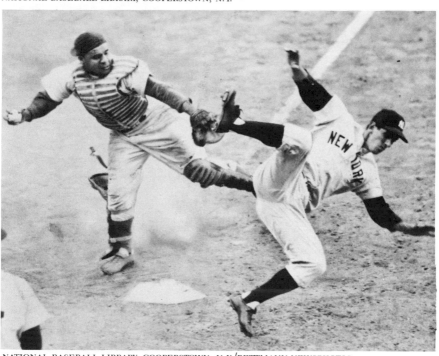

NATIONAL BASEBALL LIBRARY, COOPERSTOWN, N.Y.

WIDE WORLD PHOTOS

Joe DiMaggio idolized me. See how he is ignoring my fellow Northern Californian, Jackie Jensen, the former all-American football star? Joe always could tell class.

That large group of Yankees out of pinstripes on the lower left after they appeared before the grand jury following the Copacabana Incident includes Mickey Mantle, Whitey Ford, Yogi Berra, Hank Bauer and his wife and Johnny Kucks. Notice who is missing? I told you I was innocent.

I roomed with Phil Rizzuto in 1950, the year he was named American League MVP. Moments like the one pictured at the left show how I made Scooter what he is today. That's Ralph Houk and Charlie Silvera behind us.

Below, Hank Bauer, Yogi Berra and Joe Collins celebrate with me after another World Series victory.

My best friend Mickey Mantle is the greatest player I have ever seen. Nobody combines his power and speed. When I first met Mick, he was a country boy who didn't even know how to drink. I had to show him a lot of things, like what a baseball was (below left). After Whitey Ford got out of the Army, we became the Three Musketeers of the Yankees—Whitey, Mickey and me. They kept telling me I would eventually grow into my nose (below right).

MARK MENDIZZA

Here I am on Opening Day of the 1983 season. That's my daughter Kelly on the right and my girlfriend Jill Guiver on the left.

JILL GUIVER

Every now and then I get some time off. This is a shot of my son Billy Joe waterskiing with me in Texas.

Three of my favorite Yankees and three of the best players to put on a uniform. If I had to win one game, I'd take my chances with Ron Guidry (above). The late Thurman Munson was like a son to me (below left). I still think about him often. He was the best catcher I have seen because of his intelligence and his competitiveness. Before he is finished, Don Mattingly (below right) is going to rank with the all-time greats of the game.

13

I have a confession to make. I have had pitchers who have thrown the spitball. My pitching coach,
Art Fowler, has taught our pitchers how to throw the
spitball. What's more, we have encouraged our pitchers
to use it in a game.

I'm not going to tell you who, when or where
because some of those pitchers are still pitching and
still using the spitter, and I don't want to take bread out
of their mouths. I even managed against some of the
pitchers who used the spitter when they pitched for
me, and I knew they were using it against me. But you
don't blow the whistle on them, even when they are
pitching against you. It's just not done; sort of honor
among thieves.

I admit we use the spitter, but not as much as some people think. There aren't very many pitchers who are throwing spitters or scuffing up the ball. That's because the spitter is too difficult to control and too difficult to learn and it's also because pitchers have so many other pitches that are difficult to hit that they don't need to throw the spitter.

But those who have used it and used it effectively are well known. It's common knowledge that Gaylord Perry was successful because of the spitter. The guy spent most of his time denying he used the spitball, then he wrote a book titled *Me and the Spitter.*

Lew Burdette, who pitched for the Milwaukee Braves in the 1950s, is another well-known spitball pitcher. Also Don Drysdale, although when he was accused of it he denied it.

"My mother taught me never to put my dirty fingers in my mouth," said Big D.

Art Fowler was an expert at teaching pitchers to throw the spitball. Why not? He used it himself in his career. How do you think he managed to pitch in the minor leagues until he was forty-nine years old?

Art also taught the dry spitter. He could show pitchers how to hold the ball so that it sailed and dipped just like a spitter, and it was perfectly legal. You don't need saliva, K-Y jelly, resin, pine tar, mud or any of those things pitchers have used to make the ball do tricks. You don't have to nick the baseball, scuff it, scratch it or raise a seam. All you need is your fingers.

The pitcher simply holds the baseball between the seams, without touching any of the stitches. All he touches is the smooth leather surface of the ball. The pitcher throws the baseball like a fastball, but he opens his hand upon release, and the ball sails and dips and darts just like a spitter. The hitter swings and misses as the ball dips under his bat and he's convinced the pitcher threw him a spitter. He goes back to his bench and tells his manager and his teammates that the pitcher threw him a hell of a spitter. The pitcher didn't. But the hitter thinks he did. Now the whole opposing team thinks he did. And that's almost as good as actually throwing it because it gets the hitters to think about it and worry about it and look for it, which is all the edge a good pitcher needs.

We used the legal spitter and we also used the illegal spitter. Sure we did. We taught it because other pitchers were using it and if you can't beat them, join them. There have been pitchers who have used K-Y jelly, Vaseline or mud. There are so many things going on out there on the mound it isn't funny. Roughing up the ball, fingernails, sandpaper, emery boards, thumbtacks.

Some guys set up shop on the mound like they are the corner hardware store. If they had one of those airport metal detectors on the mound, some pitchers wouldn't pass. They'd set off the loudest alarm you ever heard.

When he was with the Seattle Mariners, Rick Honeycutt was caught with a thumbtack on his glove that he would use to nick the ball. Don Sutton has been accused of scuffing the baseball with sandpaper that he hides in his glove or somewhere on his uniform. And my buddy Whitey Ford has admitted that, late in his career, he threw the mudball and he had a ring that had a sharpened edge and he would use it to nick the baseball.

When Cookie Lavagetto came down from the major leagues to play with us in Oakland in 1948, he told me so many stories about how he would cheat on the ball field. He used to have his belt buckle sharpened, and when they would throw the ball around the infield after an out, it would end up with Cookie at third base. Before he returned it to the pitcher, Cookie would run the ball along his sharpened belt buckle and leave a nice little nick for the pitcher.

If the ball is held with the nick to the right, when released by a right-handed pitcher the ball will sail up and in to a right-handed hitter. If it is held with the nick to the left, it will dip and dart down and away from a right-handed hitter. Naturally, the reverse is true if it is thrown by a left-handed pitcher.

It has something to do with a law of aerodynamics that I don't really understand. But you don't have to be a graduate of MIT to throw a spitter or a roughed-up baseball effectively.

Cookie had another trick. If he wasn't playing, he would sit in the stands with an old hat covering his face to disguise himself, and with a pair of binoculars he would pick up the catcher's signs and relay them to the hitters. That's another area of cheating that has become very sophisticated in baseball. Teams have been known to plant a man in the center-field seats with binoculars to pick up the catcher's signs. I know of one case where the guy in center field wore white shoes or sneakers. If the batter saw one white shoe, it meant the catcher had called for a fastball. Two white shoes, the catcher had called for a curve. You can only do this on a day when the ballpark isn't very crowded.

Some hitters love to get the signs. Mickey Mantle, for instance. If he knew what was coming, Mickey would just sit on the pitch and crush it. But Mickey never really needed any help to crush a pitch. I needed all the help I could get, but I never liked to get the signs. I found it made me too impatient as a hitter when I knew what was coming. I would jump out at the

pitch instead of waiting on the ball the way a good
hitter must, and it would mess up my swing. I was
always a better hitter when I didn't get the signs, so if a
coach, or a teammate on second base, wanted to tell me
what was coming, I'd just say, "No, thanks."

All of these things have been going on in baseball for years. Cheating is as much a part of the game as
scorecards and hot dogs, although I really don't look
upon it as cheating as much as getting any edge you
can. Everybody does it. If you don't, you're at a disadvantage.

That's something I could never get Roy Eisenhardt, my owner in Oakland, to understand. Roy is a
very honorable man. Too honest to be a baseball owner.
What a pair we were.

One day in 1982, I got thrown out of a game
against the Seattle Mariners, so I went to my office,
turned on the television and had an open telephone
line to our dugout, where my third base coach, Clete
Boyer, was managing in my absence.

Roy walks into my office and he sees me on the
phone.

"What are you doing, Billy?"

"I'm managing the game, Roy. What do you
think I'm doing?"

"Oh, no, Billy. That's not right. You were
thrown out of this game. I don't want you doing that."

"O.K., Roy. If that's how you feel."

I told Clete to hang up the phone and said that
I'd call him later. I showered and dressed in my street
clothes, then I went to a nearby Holiday Inn. To the bar.
The game was on television in the bar. I got on the
telephone and called the ballpark.

"This is Billy Martin," I told the operator.

"Will you please connect me with the home-team dug-out?"

"Yes, sir, Mr. Martin."

The next voice I heard was Clete Boyer's.

"Clete, it's Billy. Keep this line open."

And now I'm sitting in my favorite bar, having a drink and managing against the Seattle Mariners.

Sometimes when your pitcher is throwing the spitter, the other manager or the hitters will bitch and moan to the umpire. But most umpires can't tell the difference between a spitter and a sinker.

"Oh, that's a sinker," the umpire will say.

Umpires don't know the difference. And even if they did, they would have a hard time proving that a pitcher is throwing it. They can't stop it. Pitchers are too smart for them and there's so little stuff you have to use to make it work that it's hard to detect. Often, by the time the umpire gets the ball back, whatever was put on the ball is gone.

Pitchers will load up by putting stuff on their eyebrows, in their hair, on the hair on their chest, on their wrists, all over. And there's no rule that says you can't walk off the mound and go to your mouth. All you have to do is wipe it off. But a pitcher can pick up the resin bag with his thumb and ring finger, instead of his index and middle fingers, where the stuff is. It appears that he's holding the resin bag where he had wet his fingers, but he's not.

Umpires don't even see it. They don't want to see it. So if they're not going to call it, you're wasting your time by complaining about it. You only manage to get the umpire mad at you for pointing it out to him.

Some people believe that throwing the spitter causes sore arms. They think it requires an unnatural motion or that it takes extra effort to throw it. That's not so. The spitter is thrown with the same motion as a fastball or a sinker. The only difference is that it reacts differently when it gets to the batter because of the substance on it, so why should it cause sore arms?

Other pitches are much tougher on the arm than the spitter, such as the forkball, the knuckleball, the screwball, even the slider.

I think the screwball takes more out of the arm than any other pitch in baseball. That's because it's thrown with an unnatural motion. You have to kind of twist your arm counterclockwise as you release the ball and that puts a great strain on the arm, especially the elbow.

The knuckleball doesn't exactly hurt your arm, but it causes pitchers to lose their fastball. You have to tense up your forearm and wrist to throw the knuckleball and that will eventually affect your fastball, which is thrown with a loose wrist. The grip of the knuckleball and the strength of your fingers are what make a knuckleball do the tricks it does. That's why there are so few knuckleball pitchers—because you have to have especially strong fingers, you have to learn the proper grip. It's hard to throw and it's even harder to control, and once you start throwing the knuckleball, your fastball is going to suffer.

But as far as causing damage to the arm, no. Knuckleball pitchers can pitch for years because they're not throwing the ball with that much velocity and so they're not putting a strain on their shoulder. That's why you have Phil Niekro pitching at age forty-seven and Bobo Newsom, who pitched until he was forty-six.

The Washington Senators had a pitching staff in the 1940s that was made up of four knuckleball pitchers: Dutch Leonard, who pitched until he was forty-four; Johnny Niggeling, who pitched until he was forty-three; Mickey Haefner, who pitched until he was thirty-eight; and Roger Wolff, who pitched until he was thirty-six. I'm happy to say they were all out of the league by the time I got to the Yankees.

No doubt the greatest knuckleball pitcher of all was Hoyt Wilhelm, who pitched twenty-one years in the big leagues, appeared in 1,070 games, more than any other pitcher in history, and made the Hall of Fame. He quit after the 1972 season, at the age of forty-nine. But Hoyt told me it wasn't because he couldn't pitch anymore or that his arm bothered him. The reason he quit, Hoyt said, is that his reflexes had slowed so much he was afraid of getting hit with a line drive back to the mound.

I'm not in favor of trick pitches for young pitchers, and that includes the spitter. Those things they can pick up later in their careers. I like to see young pitchers throw mostly fastballs and sinkers, with an occasional curve or slider. Not both a curve and a slider. Either one or the other. Most pitching coaches will tell you that if you throw both a curve and a slider, it will hurt both pitches. So stick with one or the other.

The thing I look for in a young pitcher is not velocity. That's important, but to me it's only about the second or third most important thing. What I look for in a young pitcher is what's in his heart and his head. That's more important than stuff because you know they're going to go out there on the mound and give you that little extra—more than a guy with more ability who doesn't have the stomach or the head. This is what I think a manager really has to read in a player.

You hear a lot these days about the split-fingered fastball. I admit I don't know very much about it except that it's nothing new. They've been throwing it for years. It used to be a forkball, now it's the split-fingered fastball, which is really only a variation on the forkball.

The reason you hear so much about it is that a few pitchers had success throwing it, so everybody followed. Baseball is the most imitative thing there is. If somebody has success wearing a batting glove, the next thing you know, everybody is wearing a batting glove. If somebody would come along and be successful wearing mittens, everybody would be wearing mittens when they hit.

That's the split-fingered fastball. It's a fad, like crew cuts, long hair, beards, mustaches, Hula-Hoops. And it was something new. Once hitters see enough of them and they begin to learn how to hit the pitch, that will be the end of the split-fingered fastball. It will run its course like all fads.

Some people say throwing the split-fingered fastball hurts a pitching arm. I can't say. The pitch hasn't been around long enough to determine what effect it has on the arm. I think there is a possibility that it could eventually cause problems with the rotator cuff.

That's why the spitter is here to stay. It's safe. It's effective. It's hard to detect. And umpires rarely call it. Now you know why I always had pitchers who threw it. And you also know that if, and when, I manage again, at least some of my pitchers will be throwing the spitter. Which ones? I'll never tell.

14

Midway in the 1985 season, I decided to move Don Mattingly up to the second spot in the batting order against some pitchers and that really brought the critics and second-guessers out in full force. You would have thought I had made Babe Ruth a leadoff man . . . which might not have been such a bad idea, come to think of it.

Seriously, the reason people began to question me for batting Mattingly second is that he was by far our best hitter, batting around .350 at the time and leading our club in home runs and RBIs. Normally, your best hitter bats third. Why? Again because that's the way it has always been done in baseball.

I've already told you I don't believe in doing

things the way they have always been done. Just because managers have been doing the same thing for a hundred years doesn't make it right; and it doesn't mean I have to follow them. I do things my way, as Frank Sinatra says, and I haven't exactly been a failure as a manager.

More important is trying to put together a lineup that is going to produce the most runs. There are no secrets to making out a lineup. It's an inexact science. Casey Stengel liked to have a home run hitter batting first, figuring that if he can get a home run from his leadoff man and jump out to a 1–0 lead right away, he's got a great psychological edge on the opposition. It's an old baseball adage: For every run you score, the opposition has to score two to beat you.

You would expect the leadoff man to be a Phil Rizzuto type, a contact hitter with very little power, a good bunter, a player with excellent speed and a hitter with a good eye, good discipline and a knowledge of the strike zone. You want your leadoff man to be on base for the big guys, so you'll look for someone who can get 200 hits or who draws a lot of walks.

Stengel would do things differently. He'd be a little unorthodox in that he might bat Gene Woodling or Hank Bauer first. Neither was what you would call a speed burner. Neither of them ever stole more than eight bases in a season. They would draw about 40 or 50 walks a year and they'd hit between .280 and .300 consistently every year. They could also hit the ball out of the park, Woodling averaging between 12 and 15 homers a year, Bauer between 15 and 20. You might think of them more as second-, third-, fifth- or sixth-place hitters, and Stengel did use them there. But he often batted them first.

When Roger Maris came over to the Yankees

from the Kansas City Athletics in 1960, Casey led him off in Roger's first game as a Yankee and Maris hit 2 home runs against Boston that day. Of course, not many teams can afford the luxury of leading off with a home run threat like Woodling, Bauer or Maris, but the Yankees were always so deep in hitters they could do it.

Rickey Henderson is the ideal leadoff man. He gets a lot of hits, he walks a lot and he has that great speed that makes him a threat to steal whenever he's on base. And Rickey also has outstanding power for a man his size. He hit 8 home runs leading off a game in 1986, an American League record.

When I decided to move Mattingly, we were having trouble scoring runs against certain pitchers, so I wanted to stack my best hitters at the top of the batting order, all the good hitters coming up together. A residual advantage of this is that over the course of a season you're going to get your best hitters to bat maybe thirty or forty more times.

This was my thinking in moving Mattingly to the second spot. It was so he could get more fastballs to hit. Mattingly is an outstanding fastball hitter.

Rickey Henderson was batting first and he was getting on base a lot, an average of almost twice a game in 1985. And he was stealing almost every time he reached first base, so the catchers were calling for a lot of fastballs to defend against the steal. It's easier to throw a guy out stealing when the pitcher throws a fastball than when he throws a breaking ball. Why? For one thing, the fastball naturally gets to the plate quicker than a breaking ball. For another, a fastball comes in on a straighter plane and is less likely to hit in the dirt. Some catchers have egos. They don't like to be embarrassed by having people steal on them, so they'll call for fastballs with a guy like Henderson on first just so they will have a chance to throw him out. Never mind that the hitter is expecting the fastball and has a better chance to hit it. Forget what's good for the team; the catcher is thinking about himself.

It really burns me when my catcher calls for a fastball because there's a base-stealing threat on first. I don't care if that guy steals second. I'd much rather work on the hitter and get him out than give him a pitch he can hit out of the park for two runs.

On the other hand, when I'm on the offense and I've got my best base stealer on first, I love to see the catcher call for the fastball. That's something I can capitalize on by having a good fastball hitter batting behind my best base stealer. I know the manager in the other dugout is thinking the same thing I am: "Don't throw him a fastball. Don't give him a pitch he can hit out of the park." But catchers are going to do it anyway. It's their nature.

So Rickey kept getting on base and the catchers kept calling for fastballs and it just seemed logical to me that the guy batting behind Rickey should be a good fastball hitter. That was Mattingly. The fact that he was left-handed was a bonus, because with Henderson on base, the first baseman is going to be holding him on the bag to cut down his lead. And that's going to widen the hole between the first baseman and the second baseman and give Mattingly more room to shoot through. If Mattingly does drive one through that hole, Henderson, with his speed, is going to go to third base and all of a sudden we have runners on first and third with none out in the first inning and a chance to blow the game open right away.

Another bonus was that Mattingly had suddenly blossomed into a bona fide home run threat, especially in Yankee Stadium. He would end up with 35 homers, fourth in the league, and he would lead the league with 145 runs batted in and I'd like to bet that almost half of those 145 runs he drove in were scored by Henderson. We won a lot of games by jumping out in the first inning because Rickey got on base and Mattingly homered or got a hit to keep a rally going. It doesn't matter where in the batting order or in what inning your runs are produced, just so long as you get them.

When I moved Mattingly up to second, I moved Willie Randolph down in the order, from second to sixth. I called Willie into my office and explained to him why I was moving him down in the order. Willie likes to hit at the top of the order, first or second, but I told him I needed a little more punch down at the bottom of the order and I wasn't getting it. Willie understood. He probably didn't like it, but being the kind of class guy he is and the team player that he is, he accepted it and went along with my plan without complaining.

Sometimes when he was hitting well and seeing the ball well, I'd move Willie back up to second and hit Mattingly third. Willie has one of the best eyes in the game and he's a very patient and disciplined hitter. When he's going good at the plate, he's going to get a lot of walks in addition to a lot of base hits. So, then, I would have two guys hitting ahead of Mattingly who were getting on base a lot, Henderson and Randolph.

Of course, you don't want to put these things in the paper. I get a kick out of writers sometimes. Why did you do this? Why are you doing that? I'm not going to tell them why the hell I'm doing it. Those guys on the other team can read, too. So I let the writers criticize me and second-guess me for moving Mattingly to second, but eventually when it began to pay off, the second-guessing stopped.

There isn't any great mystery to making out a batting order. Most spots are filled day in and day out by the same people. It's obvious. For example, when you have an ideal leadoff man like Rickey Henderson, you're not going to move him. Mattingly is going to bat second or third, depending on the pitcher or how the other guys are hitting. Dave Winfield is going to bat either third, fourth or fifth because, like Mattingly, he's a big RBI man.

Later, down the order, I try to alternate my left- and right-handed hitters if I can. I don't want to stack all my lefties or all my righties in a row if I can help it, because then the other manager can bring in a right-handed pitcher against the right-handed hitters or a left-handed pitcher against the left-handed hitters and I can't make a move.

I try to make out my lineup according to what the guy has been doing the last four or five days, according to who's hot and who's not, and according to who is pitching against us. In 1985, I batted Bobby Meacham ninth most of the time, even when he was on a hot streak, because he gives me good back-to-back speed with Henderson. With the designated hitter, the pitcher doesn't bat of course, so if I have Meacham hitting ninth, it's like having two leadoff men. But if I had a lot of guys in a slump and we weren't scoring runs and Meacham was especially hot, I would move him up to second for two or three days.

Sometimes, you make lineup changes just for the sake of making a change; to shake things up. Once during the 1977 season with the Yankees, we were having a tough time scoring runs, so I put the names of my nine starters in a hat, had Reggie Jackson draw the names out of the hat and batted them in the order in which their names were drawn. I wound up with Chris Chambliss, who usually batted fourth or fifth, batting eighth. And he had a big day, driving in four runs, and it helped us break a slump. We kept that lineup for about four games. It was fun, it loosened everybody up, it was a change and it might have proved that a batting order can be overrated.

Normally, what you try to do is protect yourself where you have been weak scoring runs, but I will always have my best hitters at the top half of the lineup.

As I have already discussed, your game and your lineup are dictated by your personnel.

Rickey wanted to steal more in 1985, but I kept the wraps on him. He wanted to steal on his own. Often, I'd let him. But I also told him I didn't want him sliding a lot, getting himself banged up. An injury to Henderson was something we didn't need. Besides, with Mattingly swinging a hot bat and other guys hitting home runs, it wasn't always necessary for Rickey to steal to produce a run.

I was more likely to run him early in the game, to get a first-and-third situation on a base hit, to try to get a rally going. If he steals in the first inning or the third inning and first base is open with Mattingly coming up, you know they're not going to walk Mattingly that early. Later in the game, I might give Henderson the "no steal" sign, because if he stole, then they might walk Mattingly with first base open and I didn't want to lose Mattingly's bat. I wanted them to pitch to him so that maybe he'll hit one out and we've got two quick runs.

It goes without saying that all this depends on the situation, the score, the inning, the count. So many factors dictate what you do and when you do it, but the

My baseball idol and my professional father, the Ol' Perfessor, Casey Stengel. I owe him everything. And two of the best in recent years. Earl Weaver won't be managing the 1987 season. I started out disliking Weaver, but I got to know him better, and came to like and respect him. He was the best manager I ever went up against. I'll miss him and so will baseball. Tommy Lasorda is doing one of the things he does best—talking *about* baseball—off the field.

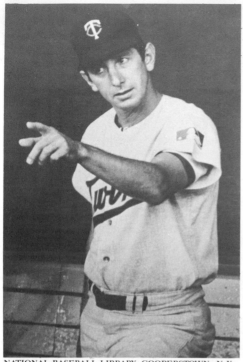

In my managerial career I've had almost as many costume changes as Liberace. I started with the Minnesota Twins (left), then the Detroit Tigers (below left), then the Texas Rangers (below), then the Yankees (upper right), then the Oakland A's (right), then the Yankees again (far right), and then the Yankees twice again. Notice the difference between my days with the Twins and the Yankees. Managing sure does age you.

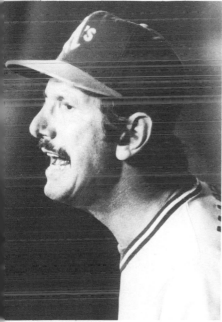

Some of the owners who hired me and fired me. Calvin Griffith (above left) was the first owner to hire me to manage his team, the Minnesota Twins. I won a division championship for him and that winter I was fired. Bob Short (above right) and Charlie Finley (below) didn't fire me, but their successors with the Texas Rangers and Oakland A's did. This is one of the few times I ever saw Charlie in the year I managed his Oakland club.

George Steinbrenner hired me...then I quit (he says he fired me)...then hired me... then fired me...then hired me...then fired me...then hired me...

As you can see, some of my best friends are
umpires. Here (above) Art Frantz and I are dis-
cussing where we should have dinner. George
Maloney and I (right) are demonstrating danc-
ing the tarantella. I'm showing Dallas Parks
(above right) the proper way to kick a field goal
using the soccer-style kick. Ken Kaiser and I (far
right) are engaged in a meaningful discussion of
the pros and cons of reforming the tax code.

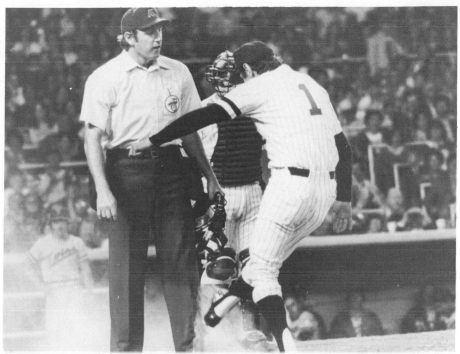

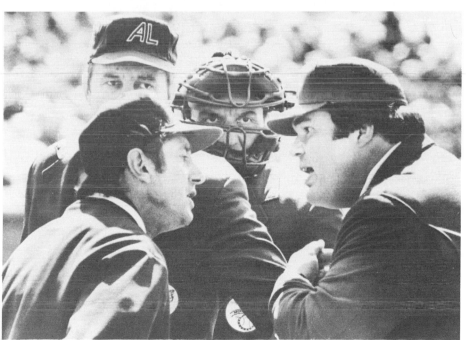

Graig Nettles (above) was on the first team I ever managed, Denver in 1968, and he was with me when we won two straight pennants with the Yankees in 1976 and 1977. Nettles has a chance to be an outstanding manager someday. He's one of the smartest ballplayers I ever had, as well as one of the three best third basemen I ever saw.

Usually, I let my pitching coach go to the mound to talk to a pitcher. Occasionally, I'll go myself when I have something specific to say—like chew the pitcher out, offer some encouragement or discuss how I want a hitter pitched. Here, Mike Norris is getting some specific advice while catcher Mike Heath takes in an earful.

bottom line for a manager on making out a lineup is this: to be able to write in the name "Mattingly" or "DiMaggio" or "Mantle" or "Mays" or "Williams" or "Musial" or "Aaron." Anywhere.

15

Baseball owners are just like people. They come in all sizes and shapes, with a variety of personalities and demeanors. I have worked for several owners and found that they ranged from the paternalistic, low-key, behind-the-scenes type of owner whom you never see to the fiery, involved, meddlesome owner who has his finger into everything. I liked some of my owners, didn't like others. Some I wouldn't hear from for months, others would be on the telephone every day, all hours of the day or night, sometimes three and four times a day. But most of them had one thing in common. They fired me. Some of them more than once.

My first owner was Calvin Griffith in Minnesota. Calvin was unique, a man whose entire life was baseball. He was a throwback to the old type of owner who did not have another business and who spent his entire time running his ball club. Most of today's owners are millionaires who made their money outside of baseball and bought into the game and I think that's one of the problems with the game today. I respect a man like Calvin Griffith whose whole life was baseball and I liked working for him.

When he was about nine years old, Calvin was adopted by Clark Griffith, one of the true pioneers of the game, a man who was affectionately known as "The Old Fox." Old man Griffith had been a player before the turn of the century and a manager of the Chicago White Sox, New York Yankees, Cincinnati Reds and Washington Senators. He eventually bought the Washington club and ran it until his death in 1955, when Calvin inherited the club and took over its operation.

Calvin was all baseball, through and through. He started working for the team when he was just a boy and he never had another job.

When the Washington club began to lose money and attendance declined for a variety of reasons, Calvin reluctantly moved his team to Minnesota in 1961. First, the St. Louis Browns had moved to Baltimore to become the Orioles and they were only about sixty miles away from Calvin's team and that cut into the Senators' territory and hurt their attendance. The Dodgers had already left Brooklyn for Los Angeles and the Giants had moved from New York to San Francisco, so the migration of baseball teams to the West was on in full force. Minnesota was virgin territory, always a good baseball area, and Calvin had the area all to himself. He drew well and made a lot of money out there in his first few years. It was a good move for Griffith, who felt he had no choice but to leave Washington and jump to Minnesota before somebody else beat him to it.

The Twins were run strictly as a family business. The Griffiths were related by marriage to Joe Cronin, the Hall of Fame shortstop and former manager and general manager of the Boston Red Sox, who later became president of the American League.

Calvin's sister was married to Joe Haynes, who had pitched in the major leagues for fourteen seasons with Washington and the Chicago White Sox. I have already mentioned that the Griffiths also were related to Sherry Robertson, an outfielder for the Senators from 1940 to 1952.

And they all worked for the Twins. The entire organization was made up of Griffiths, Robertsons and Hayneses. All relatives. But there was one nonrelative, Howard Fox, who was the traveling secretary of the team when I played there, coached there and managed there. Howard never liked me and I believe the only reason I am not with the Twins today is not Calvin Griffith; it is Howard Fox.

In 1969, my first year as a major league manager, the Twins won their division championship. We were beaten by the Baltimore Orioles in the League Championship Series, a three-game sweep. But the first two games were two of the toughest games I have ever been involved in. We lost the first game, 4–3, in twelve innings and the second game, 1–0, in eleven innings. In both games, the winning run scored with two outs. And what really burned me was that in the first game, we lost on a two-strike suicide squeeze by Paul Blair.

After the season I was fired and I know now it wasn't entirely Calvin's idea. It was something Howard Fox said that influenced him in firing me.

I don't know what it was between Howard and

me. I don't even know when it started. There just were
bad vibes between us. That happens sometimes between two people, often for no special reason.

I think it started when I played for the Twins,
and it continued when I became a coach. Even Sam
Mele, the manager, used to tell me, "Howard doesn't
like you, Billy."

Sam would be around Howard, and Howard
would bad-mouth me, and whatever he said, Sam
would tell me because Sam and I were friends. Even
when we played against each other, we were friends, so
I know that what Sam was telling me was the truth.

I do remember one specific incident that happened in 1966 when I was a coach for the Twins. There
was an airplane strike and teams were sharing planes,
flying together because of the difficulty in traveling. We
had just finished a series in Minnesota against the Yankees. We were going to Washington and the Yankees
were going home, so we shared the same plane, the
Yankees on one side of the plane, the Twins on the
other. We were going to fly to Washington, where we
would get off, then the plane would take the Yankees to
New York.

Clete Boyer, who was still with the Yankees at
the time, and a relief pitcher named Hal Reniff had a
few too many drinks and they began to get a little loud.
Howard says to me, "Go tell those Yankees to keep
quiet."

As traveling secretary of the home team, Howard was in charge of making arrangements for the
flight, so he must have thought it was his job to maintain
law and order. But why me? I wasn't even the manager,
Sam Mele was. I'm only the third base coach. Maybe
because I was an ex-Yankee and I still had friends on
that team, he thought I could control them. But it was

none of my business how they were acting, and it certainly wasn't my job to keep them under control. I told Howard as much.

"Hey, it says 'Twins' on my uniform, buddy, not 'Yankees,' " I said. "Go talk to Ralph Houk, he's their manager. Tell him to quiet them down."

I guess he didn't like that, because he gave me a dirty look.

Now we get to the hotel in Washington and we're standing in the lobby waiting to check in. It was the custom of the traveling secretary to collect the room keys and hand them out. The manager first, then the coaches, then the players. Howard gives Mele his key, then he gives all the other coaches their keys, then the players. I'm still standing there without my key. I'm there with Bob Allison and Harmon Killebrew, who were waiting to change their rooms to bigger rooms or a suite. And we're the only ones without keys.

Finally, Howard takes my key and flings it at me. It hits me in the face and splits my lip. I pick the key off the floor and I tell him, "One of these days, you're going to get your ass kicked, buddy."

Now I'm turning away to go to the elevator and I hear Howard say, "How about right now?"

So I turn around and, boom, I hit him. Knocked him cold.

I guess that's not the way to win friends and influence people and from that day on Howard carried a vendetta against me and I believe he vowed to get me fired.

The 1969 World Series was played in Baltimore. We had lost the playoffs, but I wasn't even invited to the World Series. I'm the Twins' manager, and management didn't even invite me. In Baltimore, the Twins' front office management had a meeting to go over what they were going to do with the club for the following season. And it was at that meeting that the subject of the manager came up. It was at that meeting that I was fired. I'm convinced Howard Fox talked against me at the meeting and I know that helped get me fired.

I don't know why Howard had such an influence over Calvin, but he did. You would think he knew where Calvin's skeletons were buried. Howard was Calvin's eyes, ears, nose, voice and everything else. What Howard Fox said went.

For some reason, Sherry Robertson missed that meeting in Baltimore. I think if Sherry had been there, I might not have been fired. Sherry liked me. He wanted me to remain as manager. But he wasn't there to talk in my behalf.

I talked to Calvin shortly after the meeting and he said, "We haven't made a decision yet. I don't know what I'm going to do, but whenever I make a decision, I'll call you."

He never called. A few weeks later, I was coming back from duck hunting and I heard on the radio I had been fired.

Just for the record, the year before I got there, the Twins won 79 games and finished seventh in a ten-team league. The year I was there, which was the first year of divisional play, we won 97 games and finished nine games ahead of Oakland in the American League West.

In Detroit, my owner was a man named John Fetzer. He was a very fine man, very quiet, a true gentleman in every sense of the word. Mr. Fetzer was one of those owners who remained in the background and let his baseball people run the club. It may be hard to believe nowadays, but there were owners like that.

Mr. Fetzer had made his money as the owner of several radio stations. He loved baseball, but he recognized that he lacked expertise in the game and he let others make the baseball decisions for him. He was a wonderful man and he took a liking to me and that might have caused my downfall.

I rarely talked with Mr. Fetzer or saw him, but when I did we never talked about baseball. He was really not a factor as an owner. Jim Campbell ran the club.

Jim is an outstanding individual. Soft-spoken and intelligent, he has a tendency to be a little overweight and he was always with a cigar in his hand. He rose through the ranks, from farm director of the club to general manager to president. I truly believe that when they brought me to Detroit, they intended to have me stay there for a long time. But I clashed with Campbell and I think he may have resented my relationship with Mr. Fetzer. It seemed the friendlier I got with Mr. Fetzer, the more problems I had with Jim Campbell. There might have been some thought on Jim's part that I was looking to boost myself with Mr. Fetzer with an eye to one day taking Jim's job. Jim never said so, but if that's what he thought that was far from the truth.

I have always maintained that a man has to know his limitations and I knew I wasn't cut out to run a ball club, to deal with radio and TV rights and players' contracts and stadium operations.

My expertise is in player evaluation and it was here that I clashed with Campbell. They had players there who I thought were over the hill and I told Campbell so. But he had signed a lot of these players when he was farm director and he was reluctant to get rid of them.

My first year in Detroit was 1971. I had been out of work just one year. We finished second that season and the next season we won our division and were beaten by the powerful Oakland A's club in a five-game League Championship Series.

Even though we won our division, I knew the team was getting old and I kept telling Campbell to do something.

Al Kaline was coming to the end of his great career. Bill Freehan, our catcher, batted only .234 and drove in 29 runs in 1973 and his arm was gone, he couldn't throw anybody out. I thought Jim Northrup was on the way down. So were our second baseman, Dick McAuliffe, and our shortstop, Eddie Brinkman. We had no speed. The year we won the American League East, 1972, the whole team stole 17 bases.

"Jim," I said. "These guys are over the hill. They've had it. They're gone. You have to make some trades."

He kept telling me we had some kids coming up through the farm system, but when I took a look at them in spring training, I didn't think they could play. Campbell kept touting a couple of outfielders named Ike Blessitt and Marv Lane. He said they were our outfielders of the future. I thought they were terrible. Blessitt had all of five at bats in his major league career. Lane did a little better. He played parts of five different seasons, got in ninety games and batted .207. And these were the so called great kids Campbell wanted to stick me with and I knew they wouldn't make the grade, and that eventually got me fired.

I made the mistake of telling Campbell he had problems and his star kids were bad and he didn't like hearing it, so we got into it. But I was telling him these things for his own good as well as mine. I couldn't be a yes man. I never have been and I never will be. It's not my style to tell people what they want to hear if it's wrong. Especially if it means I was putting my job and my reputation on the line, too.

In the spring of 1973, I had another clash with Campbell over Willie Horton. Willie would come late to the ballpark, he would skip batting practice, he missed the team picture. Things like that. And Campbell was making excuses for him, letting Willie think it was all right for him to pull that stuff. I told Jim I couldn't have that on my team and we had a meeting, the three of us.

Willie is sitting right there and Campbell is sticking up for him, trying to get me to allow Willie to get away with these little idiosyncrasies of his.

"Hold it," I said. "Horton is just a player like the rest of them. He's no better than any of the others. He's going to do exactly what the rest of them do. No different. No favors."

"But, Billy . . ."

"But nothing. Matter of fact, f—— you, Jim, I quit. Make Horton the manager."

And I walked out.

It was nothing personal against Willie Horton. But we were locking horns and I couldn't lose control of him or I would lose control of the rest of the team. Now Willie would go through a wall for me. I gave him a job as a coach when I came back to the Yankees in 1985. I was just trying to help him grow up back there in Detroit, that's all. I was trying to get him out of the environment he was in in Detroit and let him know that he was just one of twenty-five.

A manager has to have that kind of control over his players. And he has to have the support of his general manager and his owner in order to maintain that control.

I made another mistake. I asked Campbell for a three-year contract. I was looking for security because I didn't want to be the scapegoat when the team started going bad, as I knew it would.

"No way," he said.

Then I got a letter from Buzzie Bavasi, who was the general manager of the Los Angeles Dodgers.

"How dare you ask for a three-year contract?" Bavasi wrote. "Our manager, Walter Alston, has never had more than a one-year contract."

What business of his was it if I got a three-year contract? He was probably afraid that if I got a three-year contract, Alston would want the same thing and he wanted to put a stop to it. Still, it wasn't any of his business. I wrote Bavasi a letter and told him that I didn't need him to be sticking his nose in my business and that I didn't give a damn what Walter Alston got and he shouldn't care what I get.

I went back to Campbell and he had received a copy of the letter Bavasi sent me. I stuck to my guns.

"I want three years, Jim," I said.

"No, we're not doing it," Campbell insisted.

And that was the straw that broke the camel's back. I was fired with nineteen games left in the season and the team in third place. After I left, the Tigers didn't win the division again for eleven years. And in 1974, the year after I was fired, Campbell hired Ralph Houk and gave him a five-year contract.

Seven days after I was fired in Detroit, I went to work managing the Texas Rangers. I did it for only one reason, as a favor to my good friend Bob Short, a man I admired a great deal, and a man who has always been there for me when I needed him.

I got to know Short when I was in Minnesota. He owned the Leamington Hotel in Minneapolis, which was his home. But the hotel was only a sideline and one of his many interests.

You may know of Short as the chairman of the National Democratic Committee. He was a good friend and protégé of the late Senator Hubert H. Humphrey. Later, Short would run for Humphrey's Senate seat and be defeated.

As a noted sportsman, he had owned the Minneapolis Lakers and was instrumental in moving them to Los Angeles, where they have enjoyed great success. He was a big baseball fan and had interests in several clubs at different times, but he always wanted to own his own team. He got his chance when the American League expanded to ten teams in 1961. After the Washington Senators became the Minnesota Twins, another team was put in Washington, an expansion team also called the Senators.

They couldn't make it in Washington, either, and in 1972 they became the Texas Rangers. That's when Bob Short bought them. He kept telling me he wanted me to manage his team, but I had a job. Then, sure enough, as soon as I got fired, Bob was on the telephone asking me to go to work for him.

I had had two bad experiences as a manager, getting fired in Minnesota and getting fired in Detroit. I didn't want to go through that again. I didn't think I wanted to manage again. But Bob talked to me for four hours, begging me to take the job because it looked like he was going to lose $4 million and he felt I could help him avoid that. When he put it like that, I figured I couldn't say no to him. I owed it to him for all he did for me. So I took the job, even though I would be making the same money I made in Detroit.

I had no promise of more money, no house, nothing. But I did insist on one stipulation to be drawn up in my contract and that was that I would have the final say on personnel. I would decide who came up and who went down, and I would have something to say about trades. I felt that would help me avoid what had happened in Detroit.

Pretty soon, Short found himself low in funds and he was forced to sell the club. If he hadn't, I probably would have stayed there for years. I might still be there today.

The club was bought by Brad Corbett, who had made a bundle of money when he invented a new kind of plastic pipe. Soon after Corbett took over, he hired my old Yankee teammate Dr. Bobby Brown, now the president of the American League. Brown was a cardiologist in the Dallas area, but he gave up his practice because he wanted to get back in baseball.

You may have heard the stories about how when Bobby came up with the Yankees in the forties, they roomed him with Yogi Berra. At night, in the room, Yogi would be reading his comic books and Bobby would be reading some big medical text, like Gray's *Anatomy*. One night, Bobby closed his book with a sigh and a loud thud and Yogi is supposed to have said, "My book was good. How did yours come out?"

Bobby was brought in by Corbett to run the ball club. I had no problem with that. I liked Bobby and I respected him and trusted him. Besides, I still had that clause in my contract.

We had a young pitcher named David Clyde, whom they had signed right out of high school, and they used him to fill the ballpark, for he was a local hero, a Texan, and something of a curiosity. He had never played in the minor leagues or even in college.

He had thrown about a dozen no-hitters in high school and he was well known in the area. Comparisons were made with Bob Feller, who had stepped right off an Iowa farm to pitch in the big leagues and become one of the greatest pitchers the game has known.

Clyde had a great arm, but believe me, he was no Bob Feller. He had a chance to be a good major league pitcher, but he just wasn't ready to pitch in the big leagues. He should have gone down to the minor leagues. If he had gone down and pitched like I wanted him to, learned his trade, learned how to pitch, I am certain he would have helped the Rangers for years. But they had built him into such an attraction that he helped fill the ballpark and Corbett was shortsighted. He could see only dollar signs and packed houses. He could not see beyond today's attendance.

Another thing about going to the minor leagues: It helps a kid grow up, it helps him learn how to handle professional life. Most of these kids have never been away from home before and they need to learn how to handle that. Clyde was learning in the major leagues and he was not mature enough to handle it. He began to adopt a major league lifestyle. He was running around with players who had been in the majors for years, who had paid their dues and established themselves. They knew how to handle the life, David didn't.

The Rangers refused to send him down and that ruined the kid. Three years later, he was traded to Cleveland and he eventually faded out of baseball. He won only 18 games in the major leagues, only 7 for the Rangers. What a waste of talent. And it all could have been avoided. I kept telling Corbett to send him to the minor leagues, but he kept refusing to do it. Finally, I said to him, "You'd better get on the telephone and talk to Bob Short. I don't think you found out all the ground rules when you bought this club. Check my contract. It says I have the last say on who goes down and who doesn't."

And that was the beginning of the end for me in Texas because when Corbett found out it was in my contract that he couldn't make a move without my O.K., that caused problems between us. He told people in private that his ambition was to get rid of me and then Commissioner Bowie Kuhn. He made good on half his promise.

Corbett wanted to bring Willie Davis, the old Dodger outfielder, to the club. I was opposed to the idea. I didn't like Davis. I didn't think he could help us. He was thirty-five years old and he had lost his blazing speed and I didn't think he could play anymore. I wanted to build that club with young players. Davis was just going through the motions, picking up a paycheck.

Besides, I didn't like his attitude. I was afraid he would have a negative influence on our younger players. A guy like that can poison a clubhouse and I told Corbett how I felt.

But Corbett wanted him because Davis had been a big star for the Dodgers, he was a name player who had been in the World Series and Brad thought he could help sell some tickets. Once again, he wasn't looking beyond tonight's attendance.

"Please, Billy," Brad said. "Just let me do this one thing."

Against my better judgment, I backed down and let him sign Davis, and that was the worst thing I could have done. Davis was useless to us. He played forty-two games for the Rangers and batted .249 and they finally got rid of him by sending him to the St. Louis Cardinals. And I don't think he sold many tickets.

Who's going to buy tickets to see a .249 hitter with no power who couldn't run anymore?

I told Corbett that was the last time he was going to make a move like that, against my wishes. As long as I was there, I said, I would never allow him to do that with my ball club. That was a mistake on my part. I shouldn't have used the expression "as long as I'm here," because it gave Corbett ideas. It soon became clear that I wasn't going to be there much longer.

Don't get me wrong, I have nothing against Corbett personally, we just disagreed on some personnel decisions. Brad even came to Yankee Stadium when they retired my number. What people might not realize is that my having differences of opinion with owners, general managers, farm directors, scouts and even the press doesn't mean I don't like them. People disagree with business associates all the time, but that doesn't stop them from meeting socially. I can separate the two. Some people can't.

My problem with Corbett was that, as an owner, he was a bit too flamboyant for me. He wanted to take bows and get his name in the paper and he'd shoot off his mouth too much. He'd tell writers what deals we were working on, what was going on inside the clubhouse, and I couldn't tolerate that. I just got tired of it. But it was his first time as an owner of a baseball club and I'm sure he'd do it differently now.

I also think Corbett was envious of me. When the team started winning after being a doormat so long, I started getting all the credit and attention and I believe Brad resented that. He wanted to get the credit and the attention.

Bob Short was different. He was a pleasure to work for. We never clashed. Never argued. Not once. That's because he hired me to do a job and he let me do things my way. He let me make decisions on personnel and he never interfered. He didn't think he knew more than me.

It was because of Bob Short that Jim Sundberg got to the big leagues when he did. The Rangers' farm director at the time was Hal Keller, the brother of the great Yankee outfielder Charlie "King Kong" Keller. Hal Keller didn't know his ass from a hole in the ground about evaluating talent as far as I was concerned.

The Rangers' general manager was Danny O'Brien and he and Keller teamed up against me when I wanted to bring Sundberg up to the big club even though he had played only one season of professional baseball and that in a Class A league. O'Brien and Keller wanted me to take Ron Pruitt instead because he was farther advanced than Sundberg. At the time, Pruitt was playing for our Denver farm in the Class AAA American Association. But Pruitt wasn't as good a catcher as Sundberg, even then, and he never would be.

Keller argued that a kid can't jump from Class A to the big leagues, which is something farm directors have been saying for years. Al Kaline went from high school to the big leagues, but a kid can't go from Class A to the majors. That makes me laugh.

"Why are you picking Sundberg over Pruitt?" O'Brien asked.

"Well," I said, "he can run better, throw better, handle pitchers better and he's a better hitter and a better receiver. Other than that, no reason."

I got to keep Sundberg only because I reminded O'Brien of my deal with Short. Sunny went on to become an outstanding major league catcher. For several years, he was regarded as the best defensive catcher in the American League. I don't want to say he would not have made it to the major leagues otherwise, but you never can tell what might have happened if he didn't come up when he did. That's why I say Bob Short was responsible for Sundberg getting to the major leagues.

The Rangers finally did bring Pruitt up after I left. He played in 17 games for them, then they sent him to Cleveland. He lasted nine years in the majors and had a respectable lifetime average of .269. But he was never more than a backup catcher and part-time outfielder and infielder. In those nine years, he appeared in only 341 games, an average of about 40 games a season.

Jim Sundberg, in case you didn't know, was still playing in the majors in 1986.

I was fired in Texas on July 20, 1975. I had taken the Rangers from last in their division in 1973 to second in 1974, but in 1975 we slipped under .500 and that was all the excuse Corbett needed to replace me.

I was out of work only eleven days. I left Texas and went right to Grand Junction, Colorado, on a fishing trip. My father-in-law called me and told me the Yankees were burning up the wires looking for me. Birdie Tebbetts, who had managed in Cincinnati, Milwaukee and Cleveland, was scouting for them and he was the contact.

"Boy," he kept saying, "have we got a deal for you, Billy. You're going to make millions and millions of dollars."

When I finally met with Tebbetts, it turned out the Yankees were offering the same money I had made in Detroit and Texas.

We met in a hotel suite in Denver, and when I told Tebbetts I had to have more money, he said, "Let me get back on the phone. I have to talk to Gabe Paul [then president of the Yankees]."

So Birdie got on the phone and talked with Gabe, who I assumed was back in New York. Later, I found out that Gabe wasn't in New York at all. He was in the next room, listening to the entire conversation. That really pissed me off and I told them it was no deal. But Bob Short talked me into it. He called me and told me he thought it would be good for me to go to New York and I agreed to take the job, but only because of Bob Short, because I knew he always cared for me and wanted what was best for me and I trusted him.

Between stints with the Yankees, there was Oakland and Charlie Finley. That was an experience. Charlie knew he was going to sell the ball club, so he was operating on a shoestring. He didn't want to pay me what I was making in New York, so he worked out a deal with the Yankees where he would get me for the minimum and most of my salary would be paid by New York. And Charlie didn't want to get me any players. He told me the club was bad and he refused to do anything to help me. Not out of spite, but because he was going to sell the team anyway and he didn't want to spend any more money than he had to.

"You're not going to have this and you're not going to have that," Finley kept saying.

"O.K., Charlie," I said. "You want me to take over your club, I'll take it over and I'll do the best I can with what I have."

I figured it would be good for me. I'd be near home, near my mother. She was getting on in years and it would give me a chance to spend some time with her, which I rarely had a chance to do because of all my traveling since I went away to play ball.

"Now, remember, Billy," Charlie kept saying,

"you have kids who can't play. They can't do this, they can't do that."

"That's all right, Charlie," I said. "I'll mold them. I'll make them into ballplayers. We'll be all right. Will I have complete control on personnel?"

"Yes," he said. "You'll have complete say."

"Good," I said. "Let's go."

So I reported to spring training and Finley didn't even show up. Never saw him. If I wanted to make a move, I just called him and told him what I was going to do and he said it was O.K., provided it didn't cost him any money.

He wanted me to cut Dave McKay, a switch-hitting infielder we had acquired from Toronto, because Dave had been in the big leagues a few years and he was making more than the minimum and Charlie wanted to replace him with a rookie to save a few dollars. I begged Finley to let me keep McKay. I told him he could play a couple of positions and switch-hit and I needed him. Finley reluctantly agreed to let me keep McKay and he became one of the A's best infielders for about four years.

It was in my deal that Mickey Morabito, who had been with me in New York as publicity director of the Yankees, would join me in Oakland. But Finley was afraid to let me bring Mickey out there because he didn't want to incur George Steinbrenner's wrath. So Morabito had to submit his resignation to George and then Finley would hire him.

Spring training ended and we opened the season and we started winning, but Finley never came to the games. He stayed in Chicago running his insurance business, or at his home in Indiana, and he would listen to the games on the radio and he would call me every once in a while. He heard that we stole eight bases one day and he couldn't believe it.

"You stole eight bases today?"

"That's right, Charlie."

"You stole home twice?"

"Yeah, Charlie."

"Jesus, how come you're not all excited?"

"Because they're just playing good baseball, Charlie. What's to get excited about?"

A couple of days later, he called me again.

"You stole five more bases? You guys are winning? What the hell's happening out there?"

He just couldn't believe that we had such good players, that this was the same team he told me was going to be so bad.

You have to give Finley a lot of credit. He was a smart man. Everybody laughed at him, thought he was a clown or a buffoon. He would call up every general manager in baseball every day and ask all these questions and they thought he was dumb. But while they were laughing at him, he was picking their brains. He was taking all the information they got from their scouts and he was using it so he wouldn't have to hire so many scouts of his own. And then he would take the information those general managers gave him without realizing it and he would fleece them in deals. They would give him the information and then they would get taken. How dumb is that?

Charlie was brilliant about baseball. He made some of the greatest deals and he built up a farm system by signing great young players. I'm convinced that if Bowie Kuhn hadn't stopped him from selling off some of his best players and he didn't have to unload the team because he needed the money, Charlie Finley would have built a dynasty in Oakland that would have

190   BILLYBALL

rivaled the great Yankee dynasties of the past. Look at the players he signed, the trades he made. There are former Oakland players all over the major leagues, starring in the game even today.

I liked working for Charlie. He was the only owner who never bothered me. Can you believe it? This man who had a reputation for changing managers like he changes shirts, for telephoning the dugout during a game and telling his managers what moves to make, and he never bothered me. Not once. For one thing, we were winning and our attendance was up, so what could he say? Charlie was smart enough to leave well enough alone.

For another, he knew he was going to sell the team, so he had lost some of his drive.

Then he sold the team for $12.5 million. I asked him for some money after he sold the club. I figured I had earned it. I built up the value of his players. Attendance soared to 1.7 million, the highest in Oakland's history. The price of his club went from $8 million to $12.5 million. I figured I had helped Finley make another $4.5 million. Don't you think I should have been entitled to some of it?

"Billy," Finley said, "believe me, you're lucky to have a job. Nobody wanted to hire you."

Finley sold the club to a group headed by Roy Eisenhardt and his brother-in-law, Wally Haas. Wally's father was the founder of Levi's jeans. They had a lot of money, but they wanted to run the ball club like a corporate business and you just can't do that in baseball. Baseball is not like any other business.

My attorney, Judge Eddie Sapir, still has the contract with Oakland. I was going to be general manager for five years and they even gave me a house to live in for ten years. Why did they do that if they didn't intend to keep me?

Unfortunately, that clause in the contract was never signed. We just had a handshake, a gentleman's agreement.

I had been telling Roy he couldn't run his ball club the way he ran his business, like a corporation. I told him not to go into the free agent draft because we had a super farm system and it was going to begin producing in just a few years. We had seven farm teams and, in my last year there, six of them won league championships and the other one finished second.

We had kids coming along who I thought were going to be the nucleus of our ball club in the future and some of them are in Oakland right now. I told him that's the way to build a ball club, through the farm system, not with overpriced, spoiled free agents who would cost a lot of money and still might not produce, who had already formed their habits. I wanted eager young kids I could mold my way, who were determined and anxious to learn and whom I could teach how to play my kind of baseball. BillyBall.

"Do it this way, Roy," I argued. "You'll not only save money, you'll be better off in the long run."

But he wouldn't listen to me and eventually he fired me.

I arrived in Oakland in 1980. The previous year, their attendance was an atrocious 306,763. In my first year, we drew 842,259. In 1981, we drew 1,311,761, even though we lost a third of the season because of the strike. Then we hit the all-time Oakland record, 1,735,489, in 1982. The following year, after I was gone, attendance slipped to 1,294,941. Since then, the club has been losing $10 million a year.

16

I am sure you have noticed that I skipped right over George Steinbrenner in my discussion of the owners I have worked for. Did you think that was an oversight? Did you think I was going to ignore George out of pique? Or that I was going to gloss over him because I work for him now and I don't want to jeopardize my position with him? If you thought any of those things, you don't know Billy Martin very well.

I simply didn't think it was fair to George to lump him with all my other owners, not after all we have been through together. George has to have a chapter all to himself. He would never forgive me if he didn't.

You might remember I said earlier that there

are two Billy Martins, just as there are two Howard Cosells. Talk about split personalities; there are at least *six* George Steinbrenners.

There is the demanding, hard-driving Boss Steinbrenner; the considerate, charming and compassionate George Steinbrenner; the spiteful, vindictive Steinbrenner; the sensitive, helpful, charity-minded Steinbrenner.

There is the George Steinbrenner who is a fierce competitor with an insatiable desire to win, and the George Steinbrenner with just as insatiable a desire to be liked.

All these personalities wrapped up into one complex individual, a man who is brilliant in business and a bundle of energy. You have to be brilliant and you have to be tireless to be involved in as many things as he is on a daily basis, and to stay on top of them all.

Sometimes George is not honest with George Steinbrenner. He often acts impulsively, then his conscience and his compassion for people get the better of him and he is overcome with guilt for his impulsive acts.

That, I believe, explains why he keeps bringing people back after he fires them. He thinks it over, has second thoughts, and he gets repentant and wants to make amends for the way he has treated people. He often shoots from the hip, then reconsiders after he sees things in the light of a new day.

In part, I believe that explains why he hired me as his manager four times, hired Gene Michael twice, Bob Lemon twice. He keeps bringing back pitching coaches he has fired. He brought Roy White back as a coach; he traded Bobby Murcer, then brought him back; he did the same with Tommy John.

I think down deep George is a good person

who means well, even though he sometimes doesn't go about things properly. There are times I like George so much I'd fight a horse for him. Then there are other times when I would like to take him and throw him right out of the nearest window.

You see, your relationship with George depends on what your position is with him at the time. After he fires someone, there isn't anything he wouldn't do for that person. He kept Bob Lemon on the payroll for life. Same with Gene Michael, until he left to become the manager of the Chicago Cubs. And Dick Howser. He fired him as manager, but gave him a tremendous financial settlement.

George has always been good to me financially *after* he fired me. My problems with him always have come while I was managing his team. And that's not true only of me; it's true of anybody who has ever worked for him.

I think the reason for the way George treats people who work for him, the reason he is so demanding of his employees, is that he is so demanding of himself.

Nobody works harder than George. Nobody puts in more hours than he does. Sure, it's his team, his business, he should work harder than anybody else; he should put in more time. But George has this old-fashioned idea that if you are paid to do a job, then you do that job; you put in your time, you do what is expected of you to get the job done. And if you don't like it, get another job. He expects people who work for him to earn their money. How can you argue with that logic?

There are a lot of good points about him and there are a lot of bad points about him. There's one good point that I especially like. He wants the Yankees to win. He wants them to be the best, and he gives his whole heart and soul for that. And to me, that's the bottom line. In that way, we're alike. We both want the Yankees to win and that's why I can never get too angry with him for too long. We both have the same end in mind, even if we have differed, disagreed, even fought over the means to that end.

George has been so good for the Yankees in so many ways. Before he bought the team, the Yankees were owned by the Columbia Broadcasting System. But CBS, with all its resources, all its corporate bureaucracy, all its money, could not turn the Yankees into champions again. CBS even turned the operation of the baseball team over to baseball people. They brought in Michael Burke to act as front man and spokesman to the press and public. To run the baseball operation, they brought in Lee MacPhail, one of the most respected baseball men in the business.

Lee had learned under his father, the flamboyant Larry MacPhail, who built winning teams in Cincinnati and Brooklyn and later teamed with Dan Topping and Del Webb to create the New York Yankee dynasty. When he was younger, Lee had worked for the Yankees as farm director and as an assistant to George Weiss. Later, he would leave and help build the Baltimore Orioles into an American League power.

When CBS hired him, Lee was working in the office of the Baseball Commissioner. Later, he would finish his baseball career as president of the American League. But he could not build the Yankees into a winning team, even with the wherewithal of CBS at his disposal.

CBS bought the team in 1964, while the Yankees were winning their fifth consecutive American League pennant and their fourteenth in the last sixteen years. In those sixteen years, they won nine world championships.

They then proceeded to go eight years without winning anything. Under CBS, the Yankees went from top to bottom. Starting in 1965, they finished sixth, tenth, ninth and fifth in a ten-team league. Then fifth, second, fourth and fourth in division play. Nothing CBS did worked.

In January 1973, CBS sold the team to a group headed by George M. Steinbrenner for $10 million, a million dollars less than the network had paid for it eight years earlier. Today, the value of the Yankees is estimated at anywhere from $150 million to $200 million.

Three years after he took over, Steinbrenner brought the Yankees another pennant—their first in twelve years. And in the space of six years under Steinbrenner's leadership, from 1976 to 1981, the Yankees won five division titles, four American League pennants and two world championships.

The Yankees signed Catfish Hunter as a free agent. Later, they would sign free agents Don Gullett, Goose Gossage and Reggie Jackson. George made trades to acquire Lou Piniella, Chris Chambliss, Bucky Dent, Willie Randolph and Mickey Rivers.

If you're a Yankee fan, I don't see how you can be anything but thankful to George Steinbrenner for returning your team to the prominence it always had, for restoring Yankee pride and dignity. Especially if you don't work for him.

Not very much was known about George M. Steinbrenner in 1973 when he bought the Yankees. He was not a New Yorker. He had been born and raised in Cleveland and as a young man he had been an Indians fan and a Yankee hater. And he had no previous experience in baseball.

In prep school and at Williams College, George was a football player and a hurdler on the track team. In the mid-fifties, he was an assistant football coach at Northwestern and Purdue and I am convinced, to this day, that football remains his favorite sport.

George's father ran a small shipbuilding company, which George inherited and turned into the American Shipbuilding Company. In the first few years under George's leadership, American Ship tripled its annual revenues. Today, its sales are well over $200 million annually.

As a young man, George owned the Cleveland Pipers in the American Basketball League. He has been a stockholder in the Chicago Bulls basketball team. He has invested in dozens of Broadway shows, owns a beautiful hotel in Tampa, a horse farm in Ocala, hundreds of racehorses, both thoroughbreds and standardbreds, and is probably involved in dozens of other businesses I don't even know about.

I didn't know much about George Steinbrenner before I went to work for him. I first met George in the early seventies when I was managing the Texas Rangers. We were introduced in a Cleveland restaurant called the Theatrical Grill. I had met him occasionally at Yankees' Old Timers' Games or at World Series or All-Star Games or the winter baseball meetings. Just a casual introduction, a handshake and a "Hello, how are you?" He seemed like a pleasant enough guy.

I was managing the Detroit Tigers when Steinbrenner took over the Yankees, then later I moved to Texas. To me he was just another owner, and I was having enough problems with my own owners. I had heard on the baseball grapevine about some of the rah-rah, college-type stuff he was doing, like ordering players to get their hair cut and giving pep talks in the clubhouse and checking to see that players wore their uniforms properly. I didn't see anything wrong with any of that. I always have been a believer in strict discipline for a ball club.

When I went to work for him, he welcomed me warmly and made me feel good about taking the job. And, of course, I was impressed and excited about his commitment to return Yankee pride and dignity. There was nothing I wanted more than that. He seemed dedicated to winning and relatively low-key. I was right about the first part. I would find out about the second part.

We had our differences in the first year or two, but nothing unusual and nothing serious. I found out you could talk to George, argue with him and score points. If you presented your argument logically, he would back down and give in. He was not much different in that first year and a half than anybody else I had worked for, but it was my impression that his love for the Yankees was far more than ego.

When I started managing for him in 1975, George would come into the clubhouse to make a speech once in a while. He hasn't done that too often in recent years, but in those early years, it was almost a regular revival meeting. He would march down, accompanied by four or five of his aides, and he would stand in the middle of the room and talk to the players like he was Pat O'Brien playing Knute Rockne. He tried to inspire them, but it was like pissing in the wind with today's players. Twenty years ago he would have been right on.

I didn't like it, but he was the owner, so what

could I do? I don't think it helped, but it didn't hurt, either.

I began to realize that George had a football mentality and I used to accuse him of that. I found out that when he coached under Lou Saban at Northwestern, they had a record of 0–8–1, and when I wanted to needle him, I would tell George that I could never figure out how they managed to get the tie.

For about a year and a half, I got along well with George. My downfall with him the first time was the result of problems I had with Reggie Jackson. You probably remember that we clashed in the dugout in Boston, and on national television, one Saturday afternoon in June 1977. I felt that Reggie didn't hustle after a ball Jim Rice hit and I just couldn't have that kind of thing on my team, superstar or not. So I pulled Reggie out of the game and he resented it. I wasn't picking on Reggie. I had done almost the same thing with Mickey Rivers during spring training.

In the dugout, we had words and we almost came to blows. My coaches Elston Howard and Yogi Berra had to pull me away. As luck would have it, the game was the "NBC Game of the Week," and the television camera picked up the confrontation. George happened to be watching and he almost went through the roof.

We had a meeting in Cleveland a few days later and I survived that crisis and patched up my differences with Jackson. But the following year, Reggie and I clashed again when he defied my orders. I wound up suspending him and he came back in Chicago and insisted to the press that he had done nothing wrong. That really pissed me off.

When Jackson was suspended, he returned to his home in California. He was to miss five games and rejoin the team in Chicago, after George and I had talked it over. He didn't like my suspending Jackson, but he supported me and he told me he had been in touch with Reggie in California and that Reggie said he had been working out. Later, when Jackson met us in Chicago, he held a press conference in front of his locker. He never even talked to me. Nothing. He talked to the press and continued to maintain his innocence.

Then I found out from Dick Howser, my third base coach, that Reggie told him he didn't work out in California like he had told George he did.

To make matters worse, it was while I was in Chicago that I learned there was talk about trading me to the White Sox. One night after our game, I had gone up to the pressroom, called the "Bards' Room," as I usually did. I liked to go there because there are always baseball people hanging around, scouts, club executives, former players, and we'd sit around having a drink, unwinding and telling stories. At these sessions, Bill Veeck, the owner of the Sox at the time, was always the center of attention. He'd sit there drinking beer, chain-smoking Newport cigarettes and flicking the ashes into a little repository he had built into his wooden leg.

It was always a pleasure being around Veeck. I respected him as a baseball man and I enjoyed listening to his opinions on baseball and his wonderful stories. It was Bill who told me about the so-called trade of managers, after he had downed about a dozen beers.

"You know I almost got you to manage my club," Veeck said.

"What?"

"That's right," he continued. "We would send Lemon [Bob Lemon, one of my former pitching coaches, was managing for Veeck at the time] to New York and you would come here."

I couldn't believe what I was hearing. Veeck went on to explain that it was all the brainstorm of Lee MacPhail, the president of the American League. I was pissed, but not at MacPhail. I truly believe Lee was acting in my best interest. He was living in New York and he was reading all that stuff in the papers about me and George and he was concerned about my relationship with George. So he came up with the idea and proposed it to Steinbrenner and Veeck.

Lee figured Lemon would be more suitable for George because he was a low-key type of manager. And he figured I would be better suited for Veeck, who was a solid baseball man and very flamboyant. It never happened, of course, because George turned it down flat.

Veeck told me he would have done it. And I often wondered what it would have been like working for a man like Veeck with his crazy promotions and wild ideas. Veeck is the guy who once sent a midget up to bat in a regulation game. (He walked on four straight pitches.) He's also the first owner to use the exploding scoreboard. He had a million and one promotions and ideas. I think I would have liked working for him, but mainly because of his baseball background. I'll say this, with me and Veeck together, it wouldn't have been dull. It might have been a lot of fun.

Of course, that's not what went through my mind when I first heard about the deal. At the time, I was really pissed to think that George was willing to trade me. I didn't know he had nothing to do with it. So it all came together for me that day in Chicago. I was in a lot of turmoil that day. And that's when I made my now infamous comment that eventually cost me my job.

I was talking with a couple of reporters at the airport in Chicago as we were waiting for the plane to take us to Kansas City, and I was really doing a slow burn over all the events of the day. I was angry with George, angry with Reggie, and that's when I made the statement that I would live to regret. It was my chance to let them both have it with one bullet and I fired away.

"One's a born liar and the other is convicted."

I told the writers I didn't care if they put that in the paper. Maybe I thought they wouldn't, I don't know, but I said it and I would regret it.

The next day my comments hit the papers . . . and the shit hit the fan.

I was told that Al Rosen, who was the team president at the time, was flying out to Kansas City to meet with me. At that point I couldn't care less about Rosen or whether he would fine me, suspend me or fire me. I decided I didn't want to listen to any of those things. I made up my mind to beat him to the punch.

It was late at night, but I called our public relations director, Mickey Morabito, in his room and asked him to come to my room. When he got there, I told him I was going to resign the next day. We sat up until two in the morning, with Morabito helping me write my resignation speech. I couldn't sleep all night long.

The next day Morabito called the writers and told them there would be an important announcement at noon on the mezzanine level of the Crown Center Hotel, where the club was staying. I arrived and read my resignation speech, but I couldn't make it all the way through to the end. I started sobbing. Phil Rizzuto was there and he put his arm around me and walked me down the stairs and out the door. Later that day, I flew to Florida.

The next day, I got a call from Doug Newton, my agent at that time. He said that George had telephoned and told him he just didn't feel right about what had happened. It bothered him that I was no longer the manager of the Yankees.

"Billy," Newton said. "He wants to bring you back as manager next year."

I thought he was joking.

"No," Doug insisted. "It's true. He wants us to meet with him in New York."

I flew to New York and Doug and I met with George in his suite at the Carlyle Hotel. It was there that George spelled out all the details. In a couple of days, the Yankees would be holding their annual Old Timers' Game. There would be a big house, a lot of nostalgia. That was the perfect time for George to spring his surprise, but it was going to be done with class.

We talked about how things would be different this time; how neither of us would talk about the other. We wouldn't deal with middlemen, we would go directly to the other if there were any problems. It was a good meeting. I was excited about what was to come.

George warned me not to say anything to anybody, because he didn't want the story to leak out. And I didn't. I was staying at the Sheraton Heights Hotel in Hasbrouck Heights, New Jersey, and Mickey Mantle had come in to stay with me. I didn't even tell him.

"Ah," he said. "I got to go to that damn Old Timers' Game tomorrow."

And I never said a word to him that I was going to be there, too. I was afraid he might have a few drinks, get loose-tongued and let it out. I love this man like a brother and it hurt me not to be able to tell him.

The next day, they sneaked me into the Stadium and into a private room, where I dressed in my Yankee uniform with No. 1 on the back. I waited in a corridor for Bob Sheppard, the public-address announcer at Yankee Stadium, to reveal the big surprise. Everybody was shocked. The fans, the players, the press, even most of the people working for Steinbrenner. George had pulled it off. George and Billy II was officially launched.

Considering everything we've been through, and how it has been documented that my relationship with him is always better when I'm not managing for him, it's understandable for people to wonder why I took the job four times. The answer is that when George presents it the way he does—"Gee, Billy, I really need you. You have to come back and manage for me. Do me a favor. Help me"—well, when he says it like that, I can't say no. I can't turn him down, because he has always been there to help me when I needed something.

My relationship with George is always better when I'm not the manager. The same goes for everybody else who has managed for him. He just can't help himself, he has to be involved. That's his nature. But that's because he has such a desire to win, because he wants to win so bad. And so do I.

I can understand how he feels and why he does certain things, but that doesn't mean we won't fight about them. When you manage for George, it's inevitable that you're going to clash with him, and that goes for anybody, not just Billy Martin.

Most of my problems and most of my fights with George have stemmed from personnel decisions, differences of opinion; two men seeking the same end, but disagreeing on the means to that end.

A lot of times our problems have been caused by others coming between us. George will hire somebody as a general manager and that general manager will suggest moves and, naturally, George will side with his general manager against me. I guess I can understand that. Why hire a guy to be your general manager if you're not going to listen to him?

Unfortunately, there has never been any continuity with the Yankees since George bought the club. He changes general managers the way he changes socks . . . or managers. In my four tenures as manager, I have had numerous general managers, including Gabe Paul, Al Rosen, Murray Cook and Clyde King.

I have never known a general manager who was infallible, whether he played the game or not. And just because he has that fancy title doesn't mean he knows more than me or any other manager. I have been in this business for forty years, maybe twice as long as some of the general managers I have had. I played the game. I was a scout. I know talent. Who's to say that a general manager knows talent better than I do? I just think so many of my problems with George could have been avoided if he would have listened to me instead of his general manager.

Take the case of Billy Sample. I inherited him as my left fielder when I came back in 1985 and he was killing me. He had one home run all season. One home run from my left fielder and that's supposed to be a power position. I kept saying, "George, get me somebody who can hit."

And George kept saying, "Clyde King says he will hit."

And I kept saying, "O.K., when?"

So I was buried with a left fielder who couldn't hit because Clyde King, the general manager, said Sample would hit and Clyde never would admit he made a mistake.

We had another general manager, Murray Cook. Nice guy. But I didn't think he was a good general manager. I didn't think he knew talent. Murray never played in the big leagues. George hired him away from the Pittsburgh Pirates, where he was their farm director, and made him the general manager.

At the time Cook was here, we had Jerry Mumphrey, a switch-hitter. Not the greatest center fielder in the world, but a nice kid. Very quiet and a pretty good offensive player. George didn't like him as a player and I think the reason he didn't was that Mumphrey was too quiet, he wasn't a very aggressive person. But that was just his way and despite his limitations he gave you everything he had on the field and he was never a problem in the clubhouse. I like those qualities in a player.

But Cook reached back to his Pittsburgh days and traded Mumphrey for Omar Moreno, who couldn't do a thing. He never could hit. He used to be a good fielder and he had great speed at one time, but he was getting older and he had lost a few steps and with his loss of speed, his fielding suffered. So I wind up with a player I couldn't use in place of a player I thought could help.

I kept complaining about Moreno, telling George to get rid of him and get me somebody who could play. But George kept stalling. Then, finally, he did get rid of him. A little too late. He shouldn't have been here in the first place.

Another player George didn't want was Bobby Meacham. I thought Meacham was a good prospect. He was young and he could run and I felt he had the potential to be a pretty good major league shortstop. But one night Bobby made a crucial error in the ninth inning that cost a ball game and that was it for him. The next day, he was shipped to the minor leagues.

After Meacham was sent to the minors, George told Murray Cook to get me another infielder. Cook got me Larry Milbourne, who used to be a good utility player, but when I got him he couldn't play anymore.

I told Cook I wasn't going to play him and I didn't. Two weeks went by and I didn't play Milbourne. One day I get a call from Murray Cook.

"When are you going to play Milbourne?"

"I'm not."

"Why not?"

"Because he can't play anymore, that's why. You like him, you play him in the front office. I'm not going to play him."

I would have to say that the thing about George that bugs me most is his impatience. George has never learned to understand the 162-game schedule. He tries to run his baseball team like a football team, but football teams don't play every day. They play once a week, a 16-game schedule. There's a big difference. By its nature, and the short schedule, football is an emotional game. By its nature, and the long, daily grind, baseball is not an emotional game.

Football players don't pull their socks up every day from the start of spring training in February to the end of the season in October. Because George has never played the game, he probably doesn't understand that sometimes you get tired just pulling up those socks every day. You get mentally fatigued.

You have to go through it to understand that.

You have to be out there every day to appreciate what it's like, to know what those players go through. He never did it, so it always has been a difficult thing to get across to him.

Maybe George doesn't understand what it takes out of a player to play in all those spring training games. Maybe he doesn't understand what two days off can do for a player, mentally and physically. It can seem like a two-week vacation on some desert island. Maybe he doesn't understand that sometimes it's better to give a team the day off rather than have them work out, even when they're not playing well. Maybe the reason they're not playing well is that they're tired, physically tired and mentally and emotionally drained by the long season and the traveling and playing every day without a break. Maybe he doesn't understand that one day away from baseball can be the best tonic of all.

Maybe George Steinbrenner doesn't understand that at all. And maybe he never will.

17

It must have been some higher power with a diabolical nature who arranged to drop George Steinbrenner, Reggie Jackson and me in the same place at the same time. We were together only about two full seasons, but the combination was so combustible the explosion was heard, and the tremors were felt, throughout the land.

There is no doubt in my mind that Reggie is one of the most complex individuals I have ever known. He is extremely intelligent, but he also has a childlike quality. He comes on strong with a lot of talk and bravado, but he is really very sensitive and insecure. There were times I felt he had a strong persecution complex. I found Reggie to be a split personality.

There were times I felt George was playing me against Reggie and times I felt he was playing Reggie against me. And there were times I felt Reggie was playing me against George and times I felt he was playing George against me. It was a constant, nonstop, two-year merry-go-round and I felt like I was always the man in the middle with no chance to catch the brass ring.

So much of my time with the Yankees revolved around Reggie, the good and the bad. At least one of the times I left as manager of the Yankees can be directly attributed to my relationship with Reggie Jackson. On the other hand, Reggie was an integral part of the world championship we won while I was managing the Yankees.

Let me say up front that I think Reggie Jackson belongs in the Hall of Fame. He was the most dominant player of his era, and one of the most controversial and publicized players in any era.

My relationship with Reggie is not unlike my relationship with George Steinbrenner. There are times I can see so many nice things about Reggie and I like him; and there are times he does things which just annoy the life out of me and I want to throw him out of the nearest window.

For instance, I have seen Reggie patiently stand there for an hour signing autographs. And then I have seen him be rude and curt with kids who are looking for an autograph, instead of nicely and politely telling them he doesn't have the time right now. I hate to see that because it hurts Reggie and it hurts the image of our game. Without fans, players wouldn't be able to command the big salaries they're getting and the kids are the future ticket buyers who will support the game and the players in the years ahead.

In the 1976 World Series, Reggie was working for ABC television and once when I went out to argue with an umpire, he said on national television, "I could play for a manager like that."

A few weeks later, George Steinbrenner signed Reggie Jackson as a free agent. I can't say I was ecstatic about the move. I had been urging George to sign another free agent outfielder, Joe Rudi, because I felt he was a more complete player and I felt we needed a right-handed hitter to give our team balance.

But George wanted Reggie. He saw him as big box office and, in view of subsequent events, George was right about that. I thought we could win without Reggie, but I was happy to have him with us because I knew his bat would help us, especially in Yankee Stadium, and because I liked the fact that he was a winner and he usually played hard.

Soon after Reggie signed, I knew there were going to be problems with Thurman Munson. Thurman was our leader and our best player, but he was a very sensitive person. Thurman once mentioned to me that George had told him that as long as he was a Yankee he would be the highest-paid player on the team. Then along came Reggie, and the newspapers spelled out his contract and it came to more than Munson was making.

George tried to split hairs by saying that most of Reggie's money was deferred and, in terms of annual salary, Thurman was still the highest-paid Yankee. But that line was not going to work with Thurman.

The problems for Jackson began almost from his first day in training camp. He had this superior attitude that rubbed the players the wrong way and from Day One he became the center of attention in our clubhouse. Writers came from all over to talk to him and Reggie would sit there in front of his locker, or on the bench, holding court and telling these writers how great he is, how much he's going to do for the Yankees. Here the guy hadn't even had a base hit for the Yankees and he's popping off. The other players resented it. I wasn't too thrilled about it myself.

One of the writers who came to see Jackson was from *Sport* magazine and when that article came out, after the start of the season, the shit really hit the fan. That's when Reggie made his famous statement: "I'm the straw that stirs the drink. Munson thinks he can stir it, but he can only stir it bad."

Well, as you can imagine, that really pissed Thurman off, proud as he was. And he was very popular with his teammates. He had won the American League Most Valuable Player award in 1976 and he had led us to our first pennant in twelve years and here's this Johnny-come-lately popping off about him. The rest of the team resented Jackson's remarks as much as Thurman did. Unfortunately, it forced the players to choose sides and there were not very many lining up on Jackson's side. To say that made things a little uncomfortable for Reggie is an understatement.

As for me, I didn't choose sides. I couldn't afford to. They were both my players and I had to remain neutral, at least outwardly. Inside, I leaned toward Thurman, who had been a great player for me, a tough competitor, a money player and a particular favorite of mine. I'd say that of all the players I managed, Thurman goes to the top of the list of those I liked best. He was like a son to me.

It never failed. When infield practice was over, Thurman would go into the dugout and he'd have a ball in his hands and he'd wait until I wasn't looking, then he'd fire the baseball at me and try to hit me in the legs. Then he'd run like hell, just like a little kid who knew he did something wrong, and he'd duck into the runway that leads to the clubhouse.

Thurman was special to me. The day he died was one of the saddest of my life. It was like I had lost my own son. It was a day off and I went fishing in some out-of-the-way place in New Jersey where I didn't think anybody could find me. Only Mickey Morabito, our public relations director, knew where I was and I had given him strict orders not to bother me unless it was an emergency. That's why I had an uneasy feeling when I was told I had a telephone call. It was Morabito telling me Thurman had been killed in an airplane crash. I just couldn't believe it. I had chills all through me. Then I started crying, bawling like a baby. I couldn't stop. I really miss Thurman. I think about him often, even to this day.

Inside me I knew that Jackson was wrong for those remarks about Munson and I felt for Thurman. I didn't think he deserved this kind of treatment from a guy who was new to the team. But there was nothing I could do. I couldn't take sides.

This was something that happened off the field and it wasn't in my domain, provided it didn't affect their play on the field. And it didn't. Thurman knew how I felt and he understood. He knew I had to be careful not to come down hard on Reggie for fear of losing him. We had him and we were going to have to make the best of it because the guy could help us win.

It did seem to me that Reggie was not showing any humility by making that statement and by doing nothing to patch things up. You would expect some humility, especially from someone just joining a new team. But Reggie never has been a humble person.

Later on that season, June 18 to be exact, I got into it with Reggie in Boston, and on national television.

It was a Saturday afternoon and I didn't like the way Jackson went after a ball that Jim Rice hit. I thought he dogged it and I just can't have that sort of thing on my team. I had told my players at the beginning of the season that if any of them embarrassed me on the field, I was going to embarrass them. I knew the other twenty-four players were looking to see how I was going to handle this, with Reggie being a superstar and having the big contract. I thought if I did what had to be done, that would bring George down on me. But if I let it pass, I would lose the other twenty-four players.

I knew what I had to do. I told Paul Blair to go out to right field and tell Reggie he was being replaced. I meant to teach him a lesson.

When he came into the dugout, Reggie challenged me. He kept telling me he didn't like being shown up and I replied, "If you show me up, I'll show you up." Then he swore at me and that did it, we almost came to blows. Elston Howard and Yogi Berra had to pull us apart. From that point on, the heat was really on. But we patched things up and we went on to win the pennant and Reggie was instrumental in our stretch run. Then in the playoffs, I decided not to start Reggie for the fifth game. Then we won the World Series, the Yankees' first world championship in fifteen years. And, of course, that was the Series in which Jackson hit three home runs in three consecutive at bats in the final game, one of the most spectacular and exciting performances I have ever seen on a baseball field.

I was happy for Reggie. He had been through so much during the year and now he was on top of the world, as high as a kite.

I was happy for myself, too. I had also been through so much, having almost been fired several times. I really believed our problems were behind us. I was wrong, of course, but that night we were just feeling great.

Long after the game, we were still feeling the exhilaration and excitement of winning the World Series and Reggie was still basking in the glow of his magnificent performance. I was totally drained, but I was ecstatic. It was as if Reggie didn't want to go home, he just wanted to stay in the ballpark and savor the night. It was hours after the game and most of the players had already left to go to a party, but Reggie was still dressed in his uniform and he was sitting on the couch in my office. He kept saying over and over, "I hit three home runs tonight. Do you realize that? Three home runs."

I felt happy for him.

"Yeah," I said, "and you broke my record [for extra-base hits in a World Series] and that pisses me off."

With that he started to laugh and I started to laugh and the two of us just sat there laughing. It really was an incongruous scene.

"Billy Martin," Reggie said. "I love the man. I love Billy Martin. The man did a hell of a job this year. There's nobody I'd rather play for."

Can you believe it? Only four months earlier he wanted to kill me and now he was saying there was no other manager he'd rather play for. But I always felt our disagreements brought us closer together and made us both better persons. And I felt we were going to become a great team, me and Reggie. I even told the few writers who were still left, "Next year is going to be super."

"Weak is the man who cannot accept adversity," Reggie said. "Next year, we're going to be tougher, aren't we, Skip?"

"You bet we will," I said. "We'll win it again next year."

216 BILLYBALL

"Yes, we will," Jackson said. "We'll win because we have a manager who's feisty and I'm feisty and we're going to be tougher next year. I'll go to the wall for him and he'll go to the wall for me and if anybody clashes with us, they're in trouble. We're two tough mothers."

"What if you clash with each other?" a writer asked.

"Then LOOK OUT," Jackson said, and he laughed as hard as he could and so did I.

"Hey, Skip, they're giving me a car Thursday," Jackson said. "I'd appreciate it if you would be there."

"I'll be there," I said.

"No, that's all right. It's early in the morning."

"I'll be there," I insisted, and I meant it. I was really feeling close to him that night.

Naturally, it didn't last. As that writer predicted, we clashed again in the 1978 season. I had given Reggie the bunt sign in one game. Then I took it off. Apparently, getting the bunt sign was an insult to him, but all I was trying to do was get the infield to come in so he could hit the ball past them. Instead, Reggie got insulted and when I took the bunt off, he bunted anyway, an obvious act of defiance.

That's when I suspended him. He went to California and George told me Reggie said he had been working out, but Dick Howser said Reggie told him he never picked up a baseball the whole time. Reggie came back to rejoin the club in Chicago, refusing to admit he had done anything wrong. Later that night, at O'Hare Airport, I made the remark about Reggie being a born liar and George being convicted, and that was the end for me as manager of the Yankees. The first time.

Reggie is basically not a bad person, but I always felt he put himself ahead of everybody else and that he never knew there were other people in the world. That's why Reggie Jackson could never be a true Yankee. Yankees care about other Yankees. Reggie just cared about Reggie.

He proved that with his remark about Munson. Can you imagine Mickey Mantle saying something like that about a teammate? Or Joe DiMaggio?

That's what bothered me about Jackson. He sometimes didn't hustle, especially in the outfield, and he defied orders. I felt he didn't hustle on Jim Rice's ball in Boston and he purposely ignored my hit sign and bunted when I suspended him.

When he first joined the team in the spring of 1977, Reggie came to me and told me he wanted to play as many games as possible. He said he needed a lot of work and he wanted to show his teammates he was no prima donna. So I played him in almost every game. His request, remember. Then he tells one writer, "I don't know what Martin is trying to do. Have you noticed I rarely get a day off? What's he trying to prove? That I'm just another player?"

That's the kind of thing about Reggie that always bothered me. I didn't like his attitude, his arrogance. I tried never to let it influence me when it came time to play him or not. I know he doesn't believe that, but that's his ego again. He would never admit that the team might have a better chance of winning with him on the bench, so when he was benched, he'd rationalize and say it was because Billy didn't like him, or Billy was trying to embarrass him or show him up.

When I didn't play him, it was only because I felt I had somebody else I thought could do a better job on that particular day; another player who gave me a better chance to win that game. Would I cut off my nose to spite my face? Would I not play Reggie if I thought he could help me win? Certain left-handers, he just couldn't hit, so he sat. Hey, if I benched Reggie every time I was pissed off at him, he would have played about 50 games a year.

I think the problem back then was that Jackson had come to New York, where he always wanted to play, and he wanted to prove to everybody that he was a superstar. And I was getting a lot of heat from George. So Reggie and I just naturally clashed because I hadn't wanted him and he knew Joe Rudi was my choice. I can see now that wasn't Reggie's fault. But he could have handled things better, and so could I.

Recently, somebody told me that Reggie said he could play for me again. I think he could because he now realizes he can't play the outfield and he can't do a lot of things, which I was trying to tell him all along. But he's coming to the end of the line and, like I have said, when that happens, they all suddenly mature and see things differently. It just takes some people longer than others, that's all.

I can get along with Reggie. I can talk with him. I don't dislike him. I was at a banquet with him and we talked. I'll always be friendly with him, but I can't ever respect him the way he wants to be respected. I can't because of the fact he never acted like a Yankee as far as I'm concerned.

18

October 27, 1985. I remember the day vividly.
You usually don't forget days like this. It was the afternoon of the final game of the 1985 World Series between the Kansas City Royals and the St. Louis Cardinals, but that's not the reason I remember it. I had
nothing to do with the 1985 World Series, although I
should have. We—the Yankees, I mean—should have
been in it. Look it up. We had the best winning percentage in baseball from the time I took over the team in
Texas on April 29. The record at the time was 6–10.
That's when George Steinbrenner decided to let Yogi
Berra go and brought me back as manager for the
fourth time. Or as the sportswriters liked to call it,

George and Billy IV. You know, like they count Super Bowls, Popes and World Wars.

When I took over the club, we were five games behind the Toronto Blue Jays, but we won 97 games and finished only two games behind the Blue Jays in the American League East and we were not eliminated until the next-to-the-last game of the season. I have no doubt in my mind that if I had been the manager from spring training, we would have won the division going away. And we would have beaten the Kansas City Royals in the playoffs. And then I would have been managing the seventh game of the World Series on October 27, 1985, instead of what I was doing.

What I was doing was riding in a van owned by my friend Tom Deemer, who also happened to own the motel in Newport Beach where I was living at the time. We were traveling south, tooling along U.S. Highway 5, coming from Lancaster, California, and heading toward Newport Beach. I had gone to Lancaster, which is about 180 miles north of Newport Beach, to be a judge at the world championship chili-making contest up at Tropic Gold Mine. Don't laugh. It's a big thing. They have it every year. More than 25,000 people show up and the winner gets a first-prize check for $25,000. Just for the best, and most unusual, chili recipe.

I was among a panel of twenty or thirty celebrity judges, including one of my favorite actors, Robert Mitchum, and Hugh O'Brian—Wyatt Earp on TV. Also on the panel was Peter Marshall, who at that time was the host of the television show "Hollywood Squares," and Joanne Dru, a beautiful lady who had been a movie star in the fifties and also happens to be Marshall's sister. Marshall and I had something in common. His son, Pete LaCock, played in the big leagues for nine years with the Chicago Cubs and the Kansas City Royals. In fact, he was with the Royals when we beat them in the 1977 American League Championship Series.

Anyway, we were on our way home and I was feeling pretty good, relaxed and rested. Tom had turned the television on because the seventh game of the World Series was going to start in a little while, and I heard the announcer say, "George Steinbrenner" and "Lou Piniella," and when I heard him say, "Billy Martin," that really got my attention. He was saying that the Yankees had announced that Lou Piniella would be their manager for the 1986 season. I felt like a piece of shit.

It's not that it was such a great surprise or anything, you understand. I knew I wouldn't be back to manage the Yankees in 1986, and I knew Lou Piniella was going to be my successor. That was George's plan all along and my attorney and I had agreed to that plan. That's what he told me when he brought me back in April. I was supposed to be the manager for a year, maybe two, and part of my job was to groom Piniella to be my successor. Still, when you hear it like that, from some guy on television, it kind of shocks you. Later, George told Eddie Sapir that he tried calling me to tell me directly, but that he couldn't reach me. That's possible, because I was at the chili-making contest. Hey, I know everybody thinks I was fired four times by George. It was twice, actually. The first time, I really quit. Nobody believes it, but it's true. I'm not saying I wouldn't have been fired anyway, but that time I did quit.

The first time I realized I wasn't going to be back as manager in 1986 was in the middle of September. We were just about to start a big four-game series against the Toronto Blue Jays in Yankee Stadium on September 12. We had been playing great ball at the time. We won eleven straight games before losing to Milwaukee on September 11, in the game just before the Toronto series. I knew we had Toronto on the run and they were looking over their shoulders at us. And our guys were beginning to gain confidence and momentum. They were believing in themselves, convinced they would catch the Blue Jays.

We had whittled Toronto's lead down to two and a half games with that four-game series coming up. We still had about twenty-five games left in the season, plenty of time to catch them, but I was convinced we would pass them in this four-game series and start pulling away.

As I said, we had momentum going for us, and we had confidence. Best of all, we were very relaxed going into the Toronto series because we were on a roll and we were closing ground on the Blue Jays. It seems it's always better in a pennant race to be the chaser rather than the team being chased.

As we came into that series, I was concerned that George was uptight and that it might carry over to the players. He was making a big deal about the series. Too big a deal, I thought. He had assigned extra scouts to follow the Blue Jays and he had them come back with these humongous reports that he wanted me and my coaches to read. Two big, thick books. I had my coaches come out early that day and we went over the books, but that didn't satisfy George. We had a scheduled meeting with all the players. And then we were supposed to have a meeting in his office with me and my coaches.

But I didn't want to have a special meeting with the players. That's the worst thing you can do. The players were geared up enough already. Having a big meeting was only going to put more pressure on them.

I was going to approach the series like I always did; bring the coaches in and go over how we're going to pitch each of their hitters, how we're going to position our defense. Then we'd break up into little groups—the pitching coach with the pitchers and catchers, another coach with the infielders, another with the outfielders. Small, informal groups like that, I believed, reduced the pressure on the players. I didn't want to change a thing for this series.

Look, I know how to prepare for a big series. I had been doing it for almost forty years as a player, a coach and a manager. I know how to approach big games, how to get my players to approach them. But George has this football mentality. Every game is Armageddon.

That's O.K. for football, where you play once a week and you have to get yourself charged up for every game, get yourself to an emotional pitch. It doesn't work in baseball. In baseball, you play 162 games and you can't get yourself too high for one game, or one series, especially when you have 25 games left.

But George wouldn't see it my way. He sent his general manager, Clyde King, and Bobby Murcer, who was working in the front office that year, down to my office to take the books away from me and bring them upstairs.

One of my coaches was Gene "Stick" Michael, who had served two terms as a manager for the Yankees and who had also worked side by side with Steinbrenner in the front office. He knew how George operated and, while he agreed with my approach to the series, he said why not satisfy the boss and go through with the meeting. Stick had a point, so I told George we'd be up for his meeting.

We went up to George's office, me and my

coaches, and George was waiting for us. The office is large and it is decorated in a combination baseball and nautical motif, representing Steinbrenner's two big interests—the Yankees and the American Shipbuilding Company. The wall-to-wall carpeting is Yankee blue with the NY logo in white. There are pictures on the wall of baseball scenes and autographed photos of some of George's famous friends, like Cary Grant and Kirk Douglas. Also a picture of George with Sonny Werblin and newspaper tycoon Rupert Murdoch and one of Bear Bryant.

George is a big man. Rather, he is a beefy man with a big barrel chest. He always says he's on a diet, but I know he loves sweets, like chocolate ice cream and chocolate-chip cookies, and he can never lose weight. He fights the battle of the bulge constantly . . . and never wins.

Despite his weight problem, he is meticulous and immaculate in his dress. His hair is always neatly in place and he always wears a blue shirt with a blue tie that also has the Yankee logo on it. And he seems to always wear the same navy blue blazer, but he must have dozens of them.

He's also a terrific host. He had platters of cold cuts waiting for us and the bar was well stocked and he's always encouraging his guests to "eat something" or "have a drink."

George likes to be in control at all times. He takes command of every meeting, usually doing most of the talking. When we walked in, he was sitting behind his huge desk facing these big picture windows that look out on the field. I was still steaming because I didn't even want to be there, I couldn't see the reason for it. So I walked in without saying a word and I took a seat on the edge of a couch with my back toward him.

getyhear BILLYBALL 225

"Now I want you to get with the pitchers and go over these scouting reports," George says.

"We already did that, George," I said.

"Did you talk with the outfielders?"

"We already did that, George."

"How about the infielders?"

"We did that, too, George."

"You mean you went over all this stuff?"

"Yeah, George," I said, "about four hours ago. But if you want us to go over it again so you can orchestrate it, fine, we'll just sit right here and let you do it."

"Well, Jesus, Billy," he said, "I put a lot of work into this."

"George," I said, "I'm trying to key everything down and you're trying to key everything up. You want me to talk to the players. I'm trying to make them relaxed and you're trying to stir them up. They don't need your help, George. They don't need your motivation. This is not football."

And that's the way I felt at the time. We beat the Blue Jays in the first game of the series, but then we lost the next three, and I'm convinced the reason we lost is that the players were so uptight they didn't play their game. You could see it. They were tentative in the field and they were tight at bat. There was so much emphasis on that series that the players were afraid to make a mistake. And when you're afraid to make a mistake, that's when you make them. When you try too hard, that's when you press and you don't perform the way you should. You can't play this game when you're uptight. You have to be loose and relaxed.

Another thing: If you make such a big deal of a series with three weeks of the season still remaining, what do you do to get your team up if they don't win that series? And that's exactly what happened. In fact,

George went into the press box after we lost the last game of the series and told Moss Klein of the Newark *Star-Ledger* and Murray Chass of the New York *Times* that it was all over for us; it was a great run while it lasted, but we were out of it now.

He even criticized some of the players for their failure to hit in the Toronto series.

Out of it? Shit, there were still twenty games left and we were only four and a half games out. I wasn't giving up, but George gave up. And don't forget, the players read that stuff and how do you think it affects them? If they read that the owner is giving up, how can you expect them to have any confidence? If the general says we've lost the battle, how do you expect the troops to keep on fighting?

The players never said anything. They told the press they still had a chance, but I could see that they were down. A manager can sense such things. They walk around with their heads down and they don't play with the same intensity. And sure enough, we went on to lose the next five games. That's eight straight defeats and we fell six and a half games out of first place with fourteen games to play. It wasn't the three we lost to Toronto that beat us, it was the next five. I'm sure of that because Toronto was looking over their shoulders at us, but once we lost those five, they felt like they had shaken us. But they hadn't.

Maybe I'm crazy, maybe I'm stubborn, maybe I don't know the meaning of the word "quit," but I still thought we could win after we lost those eight straight and I told the writers so. Here we were, six and a half games out with fourteen to play, and I'm saying we still have a chance. Everybody said I was crazy. The press and everybody, but I knew we had three games left with the Blue Jays, the last three games of the season.

And I knew the schedule favored us. We had to play
Baltimore and Milwaukee and we had killed them all
year. Toronto had a tougher schedule and they were
getting tired. Besides, they had a bunch of young players who had never been through a pennant race before.
We had basically a veteran team, players who knew
what it was like to go through a tough pennant race. Go
through it and win. Players like Willie Randolph, Ron
Guidry, Don Baylor, Dave Winfield. All winners.

I felt if we could get close enough to make the
final series count, we could make them sweat a little
and we could take them. Our experience would count.

And we almost did just that. We won nine of
our next 11 games and went into Toronto for those last
three games trailing by three games. We had a chance.
All we had to do was sweep them and we would finish
the season tied and force a sudden-death, one-game
playoff. It was a tall order, but at least there was a
chance. I couldn't help thinking that if we hadn't lost
the five games after the Blue Jays series, we probably
would be going into Toronto in first place.

We won the first game of the series, a Friday
night game. We were trailing, 3–2, with two outs and
none on in the top of the ninth, down to our final out of
the season. Then Butch Wynegar hit a dramatic home
run to tie it and we won it in the tenth.

I was really feeling good. We all were. Winning
a game like that, when you're down to your final out, is
the best tonic for a ball club. And it's the toughest way
to lose a game. I thought we had them. I felt we had
momentum on our side. I was certain the Blue Jays
were beginning to think it just wasn't in the cards for
them to win, and that would work in our favor. They
were going to be tight now, not us. We had the psychological edge. They had led the division all season and

now they could see it slipping away from them. They had us down, but they couldn't put us away.

We still had to beat them two more games to force a playoff, but I had no doubt we could do it. I was wrong. Joe Cowley pitched the Saturday game for us and he didn't pitch badly. But we just didn't swing the bats. Doyle Alexander kept our hitters off balance and was in complete command. They got off to an early lead and we were unable to put anything together against Alexander. We lost, 5–1, and that was it for the season.

Billy Martin didn't lose the Toronto series. George Steinbrenner didn't lose it. The Yankees as a team lost it.

I still felt that we caused Toronto to lose the playoffs to Kansas City. They had played us so hard in those last two games, and played so hard down the stretch when we were chasing them, they had nothing left for the playoffs. While we were pressing Toronto so hard at the end, the Royals had clinched earlier and were rested and ready for the playoffs.

That Saturday game was it for our season, and I knew it was it for me as Yankee manager, too.

Despite my tirade against George, I would have come back to manage again if he had asked me. But I knew he wasn't going to ask me. I had known that for weeks.

Would I have come back? Yeah! If George had asked me back, despite all the problems, despite all the unpleasantness, despite all the frustrations, I would have come back. If George had only asked me . . .

19

A couple of weeks after the announcement on television that Lou Piniella was going to be the manager of the Yankees in 1986, I sat down and wrote Lou a letter, explaining that the reason I took so long was that there had been no official word from George Steinbrenner. I congratulated Lou on his appointment and told him there were no hard feelings toward him for replacing me, that I was a Yankee and always would be a Yankee and that Yankees are loyal. The one bit of advice I gave him was: "Lou, be yourself."

I wished Piniella well in the letter and went on to say if there ever was anything I could do to help him, all he had to do was ask. I would always be available to him. Later, I reiterated all this to Lou face-to-face in Florida during spring training.

Does it surprise you to hear about such a letter? You never read about that letter in the newspapers. You know why you didn't read about it in the newspapers? Because that would destroy the image of Billy Martin that a lot of writers have spent a long time creating; an image that is not a true one because most of the writers who have built that image don't know the real Billy Martin. All they know is what they have read and heard from other writers, things passed on from writer to writer, from year to year.

You should have seen some of the things written and heard some of the things said after my number was retired. You would have thought a sacrilege had been committed. Some writers and broadcasters, who maybe show up at the ballpark about three times a season, said that I didn't deserve to have my number retired. I didn't know there were any qualifications for such a thing. I never heard of any standards or rules that have to be met to have your number retired.

I am aware that there is a certain set of qualifications to be eligible for the Hall of Fame—you have to play for ten seasons, you must be retired for at least five seasons and you have to get 75 percent of the vote of the baseball writers eligible to vote. I never expect to make the Hall of Fame. I'm not saying I deserve to. But there is no such list of qualifications that makes you eligible to have your number retired. That's something decided upon by the owner of each respective club. It's his decision, and his business, and it was George Steinbrenner's decision to retire my No. 1. I appreciate it and I tell those writers and broadcasters it's none of their business.

At the same time, some writers and broadcasters decided it was appropriate to put down my record as a player—a mere lifetime .257 hitter, they scoffed.

First of all, my number was not retired for my playing ability. Steinbrenner made that clear when he said that nobody was more of a Yankee, through and through. George also said that he wanted to do this because he believes people, in his words, "should smell the flowers while they're alive."

For another thing, the writers and broadcasters who made those disparaging remarks aren't old enough to have seen me play, so what did they know?

Most of the writers who have helped form my public image and created this ogre that Billy Martin has become have never taken the trouble to get to know me. I mean the real me. Some have not even met or talked to me. Now, I ask you, is that fair?

That's one of the reasons I was so anxious to write this book: because I want the opportunity to show that there are two Billy Martins. I'd like to get the people to know the real me. I can't meet you all, but if you see me, come up to me and say hello. You may be surprised to learn I'm not the guy you read about.

Sometimes I think my reputation has preceded me to the point that people prejudge me. I mean, I'll meet somebody for the first time and the guy will go to shake my hand and he'll hold his hand out tentatively. "Don't hit me, now," he'll say. That bothers me. It's like I'm Ty Cobb, who spiked everybody who got in his way. It bothers me because that's not the real Billy Martin. That's the creation of the media, and the media doesn't know the real Billy Martin. I'm hoping this book has given you a better idea of what the real Billy Martin is like.

In reality, there are two Billy Martins. Just as there are two Howard Cosells. There's one Howard

Cosell who's the public figure on the tube and there's another—a very private Howard Cosell whom you meet in a bar and have a drink with. I think they are two different people. One he stages and becomes and the other is the natural Howard Cosell. That's why I've always liked him as a friend, because I know the real Howard Cosell.

Similarly, there are two Billy Martins. There's one Billy Martin at the ballpark. It's like a mask comes over my face when I go to the ballpark. I don't know how it ever came about, but it happens. As soon as I get out of that car and walk to the ballpark, I become another person. It's not intentional. I don't know why or how, it just happens.

For example, I'm not a person who has ever been a perfectionist when it comes to neatness and order. In fact, I'm a bit of a slob at times. Now, all of a sudden, at the ballpark, as a manager, I become a perfectionist. Don't ask me why. It's as if it's a challenge, a thing of honor. There's nothing else that I've ever worked at as hard as my job on the ball field.

As a result, I'm sometimes a little too rough on some young writers. I don't mean to be, but I don't have any time or patience for stupid questions. I sometimes wonder why, if I do my homework, they can't do theirs. I may be rough on them, or short-tempered with them, and that creates a bad image, I know. I'll never be able to change it. This book isn't going to change it.

A lot of people don't understand. I'm a man first, then I'm a manager. I'm a human being. I'm a father. I'm a grandfather. I'm a son. I'm a brother. And I'm a Christian.

That's another thing you never read about. I go to church. All through my baseball career, I'd always go to mass on Sunday. There were always a few guys who attended mass and I'd go with them. Frank Crosetti, Gil McDougald, Joe Collins, Yogi Berra. We'd get up early on a Sunday morning, no matter what time I got in the night before, and we'd meet in the hotel lobby and walk to church in whatever town we were playing.

I still do it, even if it's services at the ballpark. Not that I go around flaunting my faith. I don't wear it on my sleeve. But I always wear a tiny gold cross in my baseball cap as an expression of my faith and to let little kids know I am a Christian.

I'm not saying this to convince you that I'm a perfect human being. I know I'm not. My language isn't always the greatest and I lose my temper more than I should. I'm not trying to justify my behavior or ask anyone to condone it, but I want people to know that I try to live the life of a good Christian.

Father Dennis Moore of St. Ambrose in Berkeley was the one who started me going to church when I was a kid. Frankly, I started going because I wanted to play on the church basketball team, but I kept going. Father Moore was a man I admired, a man I owed a great deal. I tried to repay him in some small measure after the 1953 World Series. I had been presented with a new car for being named the Most Valuable Player of the Series and I offered it to Father Moore as an expression of my gratitude for all he did for me. But he refused to accept it.

It bothers me that people don't know the real me. It's like when George proposed me for this announcing job with television station WPIX in New York. A lot of people, including some at the station, were worried about it.

Would Billy be too controversial?

Would he second-guess Lou Piniella?

Would he use the television job to campaign to be rehired as manager of the Yankees?

Would he show up for work?

Would he be sober when he showed up?

That one really burned my ass.

I resent it when people say I'm an alcoholic. I always thought an alcoholic was somebody who drinks in the morning, who will drink alone, who doesn't know when to quit. None of those things apply to me.

I never drink before a game. I never did it as a player, a coach or a manager. I do my drinking after the game is over. I don't drink in my room and I don't drink alone. I have all those bottles that the hotel puts in the manager's suite on the road. Most of them wind up going home with me, unopened.

I consider myself a social drinker. I might go to a bar, but afterwards I don't go to my room and keep drinking. And I won't stay at a bar alone and drink. Either I'll go with someone or I'll start a conversation with someone at the bar. If not, that's it, I'm gone. I never fix myself a drink in my room. Never. When I leave the bar, it's over.

I'll drink with anybody, and I can handle my drinks well, but when I know I've had too much to drink, I go to bed. I don't have to marathon it like some people and go all night.

I wasn't sure that I wanted to be a television commentator. I didn't know if I would like it, or if I was cut out for it. I worried about being so close to the game and not being directly involved in it. One thing I did know: If I did it, I would work at it and I would be good at it. If there is one thing I was confident of, it was my knowledge of baseball. I felt that I could offer something to the listeners.

I read stories that I was going to second-guess

Piniella; that I was going to have George's ear and I was going to stick a knife in Lou's back because I wanted my old job back. I resented that. People who said things like that didn't know the real Billy Martin.

I wasn't after Lou Piniella's job. I wasn't going to undermine him. I was going to speak my mind on the tube, but I wasn't going to second-guess him. I'm smarter than that.

Besides, I like Lou. I liked him when he played for me and when he coached for me. I never had any problems with him and I always considered him a loyal assistant and a friend. I wanted him to succeed and I told him that if he came to me and asked my advice on things, I would always be willing to help him. I'd be glad to have a drink with him and talk to him and advise him. I wasn't going to volunteer things, because it wasn't my place to do that. That wouldn't be right. But I'd help him if he came to me.

I'm proud to say he did. Several times during the 1986 season, when we were on the road, he'd call me and ask me to meet with him. I never initiated these meetings; he did. He would get word to me through Bill Kane, the Yankees' road secretary, and we would meet. Usually I would just let Lou do the talking. He'd talk about everything: about George, about certain players, about game strategy, about handling players, about other teams. He'd bounce things off me and I'd tell him what I thought, never suggesting specific things, just throwing out ideas for his consideration. Some he accepted, others he rejected, which was fine. The idea was for me to be a sounding board and for me to just throw out some alternatives for him to consider.

He was always very appreciative of my time. Not only did he thank me personally, but he told the press how grateful he was to me. He called me "Skip" and he told a few writers that he considered me the best manager he ever played for. That made me feel good. How are you going to root against a man like that?

Look, if George was going to fire a manager, he was going to do it on his own, with no prodding from me. Hadn't he already established that time and again? So as far as I was concerned, it wasn't going to matter if I was right there in the television booth or if I was in Timbuktu. If George was going to fire Lou, he was going to fire him.

One of the reasons I was doubtful about whether I really wanted this TV job was that I didn't want Lou to think I was looking over his shoulder and second-guessing him. Who needed that? I knew I wasn't going to, but I had to say what my eyes saw.

To try to avoid any confrontations and to stop that kind of talk, I suggested, and George agreed, that when I traveled, I should fly on my own, not on the team charter. I never took the team bus to the ballpark; I took a cab. And I stayed at a different hotel from the one the team was staying at. I didn't want to be seen by Lou, the players or the press. I didn't want to give anybody any reason to say I was interfering, talking against Lou to the players.

Still, you can't stop people from talking, and there was a lot of speculation all season that I was going to second-guess Lou and stab him in the back. Every time the Yankees went into a little slump, those stories would start and the rumors would start that I was going to come back and manage the team. I hated that. And I resented it. That's the same reason I deliberately stayed away from the team when Yogi was the manager.

I was concerned, too, about the timing. It wasn't good coming from the dugout to the announcer's booth. Others had done it, I know, like Lou Boudreau in Chicago and Jerry Coleman in San Diego, and I never remember anyone suggesting that they were going to second-guess the manager, or that they were going to stab the manager in the back so they could get their old job back. But for some reason, when I do it, that gets everybody talking.

Another reason I was doubtful about whether I really wanted this TV job was that, deep down, I believed it was a waste of my life, a waste of my talent. The thing I do best is not talking on television. The thing I do best is managing a baseball team.

20

Why was I worried about the press saying I was going to second-guess Lou Piniella on TV? I wasn't being paranoid and I wasn't imagining things. Just look at what happened the year before when I replaced Yogi Berra. I happened to say that when spring training came around, we were going to have to spend a lot of time on fundamentals. I said it looked to me like the team had not spent a whole lot of time on certain basics that spring, such as pickoff plays, pitchers covering first, defending against the bunt.

Somebody asked me a question and I answered honestly and candidly. Isn't that what they want? Honesty? Aren't they always accusing baseball people of not telling the truth? I told the truth as I saw it and I got blasted for it.

I wasn't trying to knock Yogi. But that's the way it was reported. The press was trying to pit me against Yogi, whom I have known for almost forty years and love like a brother. They forget that it was my idea to bring Yogi back to the Yankees in the first place.

Yogi had just been fired as manager of the Mets in 1975, just a few weeks before I took over as manager of the Yankees. I knew right away that I wanted Yogi with me as a coach, but I waited until the winter to discuss it with George.

"It's not right that Yogi is not a Yankee," I told George. "I don't know what the situation was, why he left here in the first place, but he belongs here. I'd like to have him as a coach."

"Fine," George said. "If you want him, go talk to him."

So I phoned Yogi and asked him to come with me as one of my coaches. At first he didn't want to. He was still bitter because the Yankees had fired him after one year as manager. Ralph Houk had been made general manager and he named Yogi to replace him as manager. Right away, there were problems. They said Yogi had a lack of communication with the players. The team fell in the standings, but he rallied them late in the year and they won the pennant. Then he lost the World Series to the Cardinals in seven games and was fired. One game away from the world championship and he got fired. No wonder he was bitter.

I understood how he felt. Whenever I get fired, I'm bitter. I crawl into a shell. I'm mad at the whole world. My best friends, my family, I don't even communicate with them.

But that was in 1964, almost twelve years earlier. And it was the last time the Yankees won anything until we won the pennant in 1976.

I tried to explain to Yogi that this was a new administration running the Yankees, that the one that fired him was gone. George Steinbrenner had nothing to do with what happened in 1964.

"Yogi," I said, "you're a Yankee. You belong here. Come back. Be with me. You can help me in the clubhouse. You can help me in the dugout."

He still didn't want to do it, but I persisted. I talked to him several times. I talked to his wife, Carmen. Finally, Yogi agreed to come, and if it hadn't been for me, he wouldn't have been here and he might never have had a chance to manage again. Yogi replaced me as manager after the 1983 season, but I don't remember anybody accusing him of sabotaging me. I know he didn't sabotage me. But when I replaced him, right away people are accusing me of sticking a knife in his back. I think maybe even Yogi began to believe it. When he replaced me, I'm sure Yogi thought I was looking over his shoulder. That's why I deliberately stayed away from the ball club. But when George called me and brought me back to manage in the early part of the 1985 season, they tried to pit me against Yogi and that really pissed me off.

All I said was that there were certain mechanics these guys were not doing that I'd like to get them to do and I'm marking these things down so that when spring training comes, I'm going to make them do them. Every manager has his own conception of how to play the game. Yogi is the easygoing, low-key type. I believe in working on details, constantly getting on the

players to perform the fundamentals so that they become second nature. I'm tough on players. Yogi is not.

I'm not saying my way is right and Yogi's way is
wrong, but it's different, and every manager has to get
his players to do things his way. My way has been very
successful for me. And Yogi's has been successful for
him.

I talked to my coaches about certain things,
like pickoff plays and bunt plays, and they told me Yogi
didn't like to do that, or Yogi didn't believe in that.
Fine. But I did, and I promised that in spring training,
we'd work on these things.

As soon as I said that, it came out that I'm
saying Yogi didn't do it right in spring training. That's
not what I was saying at all, but that's how it came out. I
was simply saying that I was going to do things differently the next spring. Little did I know I wouldn't get
the chance to do it differently because I wouldn't be
there.

I took over the club in Texas and that first
night I had a clubhouse meeting. The papers reported
that some of the players were upset about the move.
Don Baylor threw something across the room when he
heard about it. Don Mattingly knocked over a waste-
basket. Dave Winfield had some things to say.

I didn't take it personally. I understood it.
They liked Yogi and they were upset that he was fired,
especially after only sixteen games. They felt he never
had a chance to turn the season around.

Fine. They liked playing for Yogi. I didn't
blame them. He was easygoing and I was demanding.
But I had a job to do and I was going to do it, and I laid it
on the line to them in that first clubhouse meeting. I
wanted them to know I was back and things were going

to be different from that point on, whether they liked it or not.

You could hear a pin drop when I addressed the team in that first meeting. They weren't very happy to see me. I didn't care.

"I didn't fire Yogi," I said. "You did. You guys like Yogi? You liked him so much, how come you didn't play for him? I wouldn't be here right now if it wasn't for you. Let's get something straight right now. I would be home in California. I wouldn't be here. But you guys didn't do the job. You love Yogi? I love him, too. But I'm here to win. I'm here because I want to help the Yankees. I'm back because I'm a Yankee and I want to help them. You're mad because of Yogi. Fine. I respect that. You're mad at George. Good. Play and win. Winning is fun."

I asked them if they had anything to say and none of them did. Then I spotted Dale Berra, Yogi's boy, sitting in the corner, his head in his hands. I knew it was toughest on him because his father was fired. And that made it tougher on me.

"Dale," I said, "your dad and I have been friends for almost forty years. I just want you to know I didn't ask to come here, I was asked. I'm going to do a job, but I can't do it without you. Play for me and we'll get along fine."

A couple of weeks later, I asked Dale how Yogi was doing and told him to tell his dad I was going to call him. I did, but I could sense that it was a little strained, like he was believing the things he read, and that bothered me. I called again and talked with Carmen and she was just as sweet as she could be. She said this is silly, we should all get together. After all, we have been friends so long.

We never did and I think Yogi still has some bad feelings about being fired. I hope it passes.

I don't think Yogi is the kind of guy to hold a grudge, even though he was hurt by the way George fired him, after only sixteen games, and then didn't talk to him after he fired him. I don't know if that rift can ever be repaired.

Yogi is a good person. He doesn't hate anybody and nobody hates him, but he bruises easily, just like me. Normally, he has a pleasant, easy disposition. He gets along with everybody. And, of course, he has this reputation for saying funny things. Most of the funny things attributed to him he never said, and the things he has said that are funny just kind of slip out accidentally. I can vouch for two.

I was in my office in Yankee Stadium one day. It was early and I had the television on. They were showing an old movie, *The Magnificent Seven,* starring Steve McQueen. Yogi walks in and sits down on the couch and starts watching the movie. He's watching for about ten minutes. Then he says, "He must have made that movie before he died."

Another time, in spring training, I had driven to the ballpark in my new Lincoln Mark V and the moment the door closed I realized I had locked my keys inside. The parking lot at Fort Lauderdale Stadium is very small, so the attendant wants us to leave our keys in the car in case he has to move it to let someone out while we're on the field. The Mark V is burglar-proof, meaning you can't unlock the doors by the old practice of sticking a wire coat hanger down from the outside. I was beside myself. I had a problem and I didn't know how I was going to solve it.

Finally, Yogi came up with the solution. He knew I was concerned and he asked me why. When I told him, he said, "That's nothin', Billy. All you gotta do is call a blacksmith."

21

I'm not going to pick an all-time team, for this reason: I have been associated with so many outstanding players as a teammate, opponent or manager that I know I'm certain to overlook and omit somebody. Also, there are so many great players I never saw or saw only occasionally that it would be unfair to include them and just as unfair to exclude them.

Take Joe DiMaggio, for example. I know enough about what he accomplished to know he belongs on anybody's all-time team. But I saw so little of him, and I saw him so late in his career, it would be foolish of me to say he belongs on my all-time team based on what I saw. I saw Joe in the final two seasons of his career, when his skills had been eroded by age and

injuries. But even at the stage when I saw him he was
still so gifted I can easily understand why so many,
many people I know and respect call him the greatest
player they have ever seen.

I played and managed in the American
League for most of my career, which means I never got
to see very much of the great National League players,
except in World Series and All-Star Games, in spring
training and occasionally on television. How could I
judge them fairly with such limited exposure to them?

What I will present now is not an all-time
team, but a random list of the best players I have ever
seen, played with, played against, managed and managed against. You will notice that there are very few
National Leaguers included, for reasons just mentioned. With one notable exception. Willie Mays.

I saw enough of Willie in World Series and All-
Star Games and on television to know he belongs on
any list of great players. Defensively, I never saw anybody better. He was like an infielder playing the outfield the way he would charge base hits, scoop them up
with his glove hand and throw runners out in one motion. They say DiMag did the same thing when he was
younger, but I didn't see Joe then.

Mays's offensive records speak for themselves.
A .302 average for twenty-two seasons, 660 home runs,
over 3,200 hits, over 1,900 RBIs. Outstanding.

I'd say it has to be a toss-up between Mays and
Mickey Mantle for the greatest player I ever saw. How
do you choose between them? That would be like
choosing between Joe Louis and Muhammad Ali. You
couldn't go wrong no matter which one you chose.

If you force me to choose, I'd have to go with
Mickey because of how I feel about him and because I
saw much more of him than I did of Willie. Mickey

could carry a team like no other player. He would play hurt and he was such an inspiration to his teammates. Mickey had the quality of being the big man without seeming to be. He was always just one of the guys, although he really wasn't, because of his enormous ability. That's why Mickey was so great, because he could do so much on the field and he meant so much to the team off the field.

The best catcher I ever saw was Thurman Munson. It probably surprises you that I would pick Munson over Yogi Berra and Elston Howard, both great catchers. Yogi was a lot smarter than people gave him credit for. Ellie was outstanding in every phase of the game. But Thurman was more of a leader than the other two. I think that really had to do with the difference in their personalities and with the people around them.

Munson was more outgoing and aggressive than either Yogi or Ellie. Also, it would have been hard for Berra or Howard to adopt a pose of leadership when they were surrounded by players like DiMaggio, Mantle, Rizzuto, Ford, Bauer, Woodling, Raschi, Reynolds and Lopat.

Thurman, on the other hand, was a spark plug and ono of the greatest competitors I ever saw. He had great instincts for the game. He was a lot like Joe D. in that I hardly ever saw him get thrown out trying for the extra base. He wasn't fast, but he knew how to run the bases. He knew his own speed and he knew the arms of the outfielders. So he knew what he could do on the bases and what he couldn't do.

Thurman was a great student of the game. He would have made an excellent manager. He knew how to handle pitchers and he was great at calling a game. With some catchers, I had to call the game from the dugout. Not with Thurman. He knew what I wanted to do, how I wanted to pitch a hitter, and he did it. He thought like me and he was a master at setting hitters up. I rarely disagreed with his pitch selection. He was very agile behind the plate. He didn't have a great arm, but he had such a quick release that he compensated for his lack of arm strength. I never knew another catcher who could get rid of the ball so fast.

Munson was also great with pitchers. He knew when to stroke them and he knew when to chew them out and he earned their respect. He played hurt and he never alibied. The one quality I will remember most when I think of Thurman is his competitiveness and what a tough hitter he was in the clutch.

I didn't see enough of Johnny Bench to say he was better than Thurman. In recent years, the best catchers around have been Lance Parrish, Jim Sundberg and Carlton Fisk and, I guess, Gary Carter. I didn't see enough of Carter. I did see a lot of the other three. They're not in Munson's class for my money.

The best first basemen I ever saw as far as handling the glove were Vic Power and Don Mattingly. Power was a little show-offish, but he could pick it. Everything one-handed, everything flashy, which is not what you want to have kids see. But Vic was brilliant around the bag and a great showman. He was a good hitter, but not the kind of productive hitter you want in your first baseman.

When you combine hitting and fielding, you're not going to find anyone better than Don Mattingly. Already, after just three full seasons, he's breaking records that have stood for sixty years. By the time his career is ended, he's going to rank among the all-time greats at a position that has had such superstars as Lou

Gehrig, George Sisler, Bill Terry and a whole lot of others.

I remember when I took a lot of heat because I wanted to play Mattingly over Steve Kemp, who was a veteran player and had been signed by Steinbrenner as a free agent for a lot of money. But you could just see that Mattingly was a natural hitter and an outstanding defensive player, either in the outfield or at first base. You had to like him for his attitude and his approach to the game alone. He is what baseball people call a "gamer." He plays hard all the time, he wants to win, he wants to be the best and he's never satisfied. He's constantly working to improve. And he plays every game like it's the seventh game of the World Series and every at bat like it's two out in the bottom of the ninth and his team is one run down.

Donnie is a sure Hall of Famer of the future and one day his No. 23 will be retired and he will have his own monument in center field. I will be flattered and honored to be in his company.

Until Mattingly came along, Eddie Murray was the best first baseman around if you combined offense and defense, but Mattingly has passed him by.

I've never seen a better second baseman than Nellie Fox, the little White Sox star with the chew of tobacco in his cheek. He was a tough little guy, a great hitter and a sure-handed fielder. He could do it all and why he's not in the Hall of Fame, I'll never know. A great little player.

Bobby Doerr of those Red Sox teams the Yankees were always battling in the 1940s and 1950s is right up there, too. So are two guys I managed, Willie Randolph and Rod Carew. Willie is a much better fielder than Carew, by far. Nobody around turns the double play better than Willie. But Rodney obviously was a better hitter, one of the best hitters I've ever seen. And the best bunter I've ever seen.

Carew played second base only for a few years. Then, when he began to slow up a little, they moved him to first base because he was such a great hitter and you just had to find room for a bat like his.

I didn't get to see Joe Gordon until he was at the end of his career, but he certainly has to be included in any list of outstanding second basemen. And so does Bobby Richardson, the guy who replaced me as second baseman with the Yankees after I was traded. Among today's players, Frank White and Lou Whitaker are as good as they come.

At shortstop, Phil Rizzuto could do it all. A lot of guys could play shortstop, maybe even better than the Scooter. Luis Aparicio had better range. If you want to talk about fielding only, Mark Belanger was as good with the glove as any shortstop I ever saw. Probably as good as any shortstop who ever lived. When it comes to both playing shortstop and handling the bat, the Scooter belongs with the best of them. They tell me Ozzie Smith of the Cardinals may be the best who ever played the position. I can't say, I haven't seen enough of him. I know he can't hit like Rizzuto. And I also know he plays on artificial surface and he never has to handle a bad hop.

At third base I'll give you three, take your pick. Clete Boyer, Graig Nettles, Brooks Robinson. Nobody is in Brooks's class as a third baseman offensively, but defensively I put all three of them on a par. In my day, Al Rosen was the top third baseman offensively, but he was not a good defensive third baseman. The Tigers' George Kell and the Red Sox' Frank Malzone were better defensively than Rosen and they could hit. But none of them could field with my three, Boyer, Nettles,

Robinson. The National League had some good third basemen, too. In particular, I'm thinking of Eddie Mathews and Clete's older brother, Ken. But again I'm at a disadvantage because I didn't see them play often enough.

As for a pitcher, if I had to win one game? When I was a player, Vic Raschi, Allie Reynolds or Whitey Ford. Any one of them. As a manager? Mickey Lolich, Catfish Hunter in his prime, Ron Guidry. When these guys knew they had to do it, that was it. When they had to win a game, they were going to win that damn game. There was no way they were going to lose. Relief pitchers? I have been associated with four outstanding ones. Joe Page when I was a player. Sparky Lyle, Goose Gossage and Dave Righetti as a manager.

Ford had as good a curveball as I've ever seen, he had great control and he knew how to pitch. He was smart out there on the mound. Catfish Hunter was another pitcher with pinpoint control and the ability to mix up his pitches and outthink the hitters.

Guidry has that great slider and an outstanding fastball, especially for such a skinny guy. Nobody threw harder than Allie Reynolds, Goose Gossage and Joe Page. But the thing that made all of these guys such great pitchers is that they were all tremendous competitors. But I guess that's what makes pitchers great, that's what sets them above the crowd, their competitiveness. All of these guys, if you had to win a big game, or get a big out, these guys would do it.

As I said in the beginning, there have been so many great players it's hard to choose. So don't say this is Billy Martin's all-time team, because it isn't. But whatever it is, it wouldn't be complete if I didn't include Harmon Killebrew, who was a great person to have on a ball club and a great leader.

A lot of people might not realize that when I won a division title in Minnesota in 1969, Harmon was my third baseman. He had come up to the Twins as a third baseman when they were the Washington Senators. But he was never a very good fielder and he was never very quick and by the time I was managing the club in 1969, they had switched Killebrew to first base.

I had a big, left-handed-hitting first baseman named Rich Reese and I wanted to get him in the lineup because I thought he could help us with his bat. We were a little short of left-handed hitting and Reese would give us good balance. One day in spring training, I watched Harmon taking ground balls in the infield. I noticed he still had pretty good hands. Watching him gave me an idea. I was convinced my ball club would be stronger with Killebrew at third and Reese at first. The only question was whether Harmon would go along with it.

Killebrew was a big star by then and I was a rookie manager. He led the league in home runs five times. You just don't move a player like that to another position and risk embarrassing him. You treat him with the respect he has earned. You try your idea out on him in private.

I approached Harmon and told him what I wanted to do and asked him how he felt about it. He said he was all for it. Anything to help me in my first year as manager. Anything to help the team. If I thought it would help us win, he was all for it. That's why I think so highly of Harmon.

He played third and he did a hell of a job. Not only that, his bat came alive again. The year before he had been injured a lot. He had only 17 homers and 40 RBIs. As a third baseman for me in 1969, Killebrew led the major leagues with 49 homers and 140 RBIs, we won our division and Harmon was named the American League's Most Valuable Player. Reese, by the way, batted .322, had 16 homers and 69 RBIs and made a great contribution to our championship.

Graig Nettles was on the club that year and I knew it was only a matter of time before I was going to have to move him into the starting lineup. My plan for 1970 was to move Killebrew to left field and play Nettles at third. I was going to have Killebrew play some left field and some first base, but I never got the chance to do it because I was fired after the 1969 season.

Before I got fired, Calvin Griffith told me that Alvin Dark, who was managing the Cleveland Indians, was burning up the telephone wires trying to make a deal for Nettles.

"We can get So-and-so and So-and-so," Calvin would say. "They want Nettles. I think I'm going to make that deal."

"Don't do it, Calvin," I kept saying. "Nettles is going to be a great player in this league, you'll see. Whatever you do, don't trade Graig Nettles."

I was fired in November. In December, Nettles was traded to Cleveland with pitchers Dean Chance and Bob Miller and outfielder Ted Uhlaender for pitchers Luis Tiant and Stan Williams.

One other player belongs on any list of mine. Make him my third outfielder with Mantle and Mays. I'm talking about Rickey Henderson, who I think is the most exciting and the best all-around player in the game today. I believe I had something to do with Henderson becoming a Yankee. In the winter after the 1984 season I was working as a consultant to George Steinbrenner. We were in Florida at an organizational meeting and the Henderson deal had come up. It was a five-for-two deal. We were to give up four young pitchers and a young outfielder for Henderson and a young pitcher. And George was against it.

"I'm not going to give up all these guys for Rickey Henderson," and he jumped up and walked out of the meeting.

I had had Rickey in Oakland and I was in favor of making the deal. So were several of the other people in the room, but everybody was afraid to say anything. After George left, Clyde King, the general manager, turned to me.

"Billy," King said. "Can you talk to him?"

"Yeah," I said. "I'll go talk to him."

We were meeting in George's hotel in Tampa, the Bay Harbor Inn. He had a suite there and I went up and knocked on the door. Before I could even say anything, I hear George's voice say, "Come on in, Billy."

"How did you know it was me?"

"I knew you'd be coming up here," he said.

"Look, George," I said. "You have to make this deal. I know you're giving up Jay Howell and three young pitchers, but young pitchers are a dime a dozen. You can always replace them. They come along all the time. A Rickey Henderson comes along once in a lifetime. Believe me, if you get Rickey Henderson, he's going to make the difference in this whole ball club. He'll make Willie Randolph better. He'll make Don Mattingly better. He'll make Dave Winfield better. He'll help everybody. Please, George. If I'm wrong, then fire me. I feel that strongly about this trade. I know this kid that well."

"Well, if that's the way you feel," he said, "I'll do it. O.K. Call them down there and tell them to make the deal."

And so the Rickey Henderson deal was made and I'm here to tell you that Rickey is a once-in-a-lifetime player. You see very few Rickey Hendersons. You might not see another one for fifty years.

He has to be the greatest leadoff man in the history of baseball. There has never been a leadoff man like him, not with his power and speed. When I was playing, Eddie Yost of the Washington Senators was the ideal leadoff man because he got on base so many times. He'd walk anywhere from 125 to 150 times a year. And he could hit. He'd hit 11, 12, 14 home runs a year. And he'd get his 150, 160 hits a year. One year, he led the league with 135 walks, had 145 hits, 21 homers, 61 RBIs and led the league in runs scored with 115. But he didn't steal bases like Rickey, less than 10 a season. How many leadoff men do you know can bat .314, get 172 hits, score 146 runs, hit 24 homers, drive in 72 runs, get 99 walks and steal 80 bases? Only one. Rickey Henderson. And that's exactly what he did for the Yankees in 1985.

That's why I wanted the Yankees to get him. That's why I say he's the greatest leadoff man in baseball history and the best player in the game today.

I know I have left out some outstanding outfielders of my day. People like Al Kaline, Carl Yastrzemski, Frank Robinson, and some National Leaguers that I never saw much of, like Stan Musial, Roberto Clemente, Hank Aaron. All great ballplayers. But I don't have to apologize for the outfield I chose. I'll be more than satisfied to take my chances with an outfield of Mickey Mantle, Willie Mays and Rickey Henderson.

22

There is no question that the biggest problem facing baseball today is the increasing use of drugs. There are times when you read the newspapers or watch the news on television that you get the impression the game is infested with drugs. I can't say how widespread drug use is, but I do know that one player using drugs is one too many and that the game's public image has suffered greatly because of the drug problem.

I'm not here to offer any solution to the problem, mainly because I am unfamiliar with it. People wonder if a manager can detect it when one of his players is on drugs. I have tried and I couldn't.

A guy is acting funny, his performance is erratic and inconsistent, you hear rumors, so you go through the clubhouse and see if you can detect if there are drugs around. I have done that. I have tried so hard, but I could never tell.

I can say that the clubs I have managed have been relatively drug-free, but not 100 percent clean, and that's not good enough. I have had players on my teams who later were known to have a drug problem. That saddens me. I could tell by the way these players were acting that there was something funny going on, but I could never figure it out. You know why? Because I never used drugs myself, so it was difficult to finger somebody else for something I never did. I really don't know what to look for.

Nobody runs a tighter ship as a manager than my old third base coach, Dick Howser, yet he had a wholesale scandal a few years ago when four of his Kansas City players were found to be on drugs.

I talked to Dick about it and he said he never knew what was going on.

"Billy," he said, "I had no idea these players were into drugs. I did notice some personality changes, but there could be any number of reasons for that. In one case, the player's performance deteriorated drastically. In the others, there was no change."

I felt for Howser because I know it hurt him very much, being the kind of guy he is and the kind of manager he is. But if Dick couldn't detect it, how could I?

Dick was devastated. It was only a few players, but any manager would be upset if only one out of his twenty-five players was using drugs.

I'm a hard-liner on this subject. I think baseball is going to have to look deeper into the problem and I am in favor of a tougher stand against the offenders. I feel the best way to cure something like this and rid the game of drugs is to make the punishment so severe it will act as a deterrent. I'm all for giving someone a second chance, but that's it. If a player is caught using drugs, he's on probation. If he's caught a second time, suspend him for life, take his pension away. Give him one chance. No more. That will stop it. Fool me once, shame on you. Fool me twice, shame on me.

I know Commissioner Peter Ueberroth is committed to putting an end to drug use in baseball and I believe he will do it. I commend him for his stand. I have been impressed with the man in his short tenure as Commissioner. His background shows that when he sets out to accomplish something, he usually accomplishes it. When he says he's going to do something, he usually does it. I think Peter Ueberroth is the best thing to happen to baseball in the last fifty years.

I am in favor of drug testing and I don't understand the Players' Association's position on the subject. Wouldn't you think they would want what is best for their members? Instead, they're using it as a negotiating tool and I think that's a disgrace. They're playing with men's lives. This is not something to play with.

I admit I'm not an expert on this subject, but I'd like to offer the following suggestions toward finding a solution to the problem:

1. Mandatory testing of all players.

2. Give offenders a second chance; ban them for life if they are second offenders.

3. Broader education against the evils of drugs, especially in the minor leagues.

4. Stricter control over who is permitted in the clubhouse.

Professional athletes are vulnerable to pushers because they have so much time on their hands, especially on the road, and because they make more money than the average person their age. So the pushers gravitate to athletes, do them favors and infiltrate them, and the next thing you know, these guys are hooked.

I know the do-gooders are going to say that alcohol is just as serious a problem as drugs. I'm not denying that alcohol is a problem, but I don't think you can equate the two. Let's not overlook the fact that drugs are illegal and prohibition has been repealed. When you do drugs, you're breaking the law, and you're aiding and abetting those who sell illegal drugs and profit from it. You are helping organized crime.

Baseball has undergone some drastic changes in recent years, the most dramatic of which are the new, symmetrical ballparks that all seem to look alike, artificial surfaces, the designated hitter, expansion to the West Coast and the increase in the number of major league teams, and the improvement in conditions for the players to the point where they have become as powerful as the owners; a case of the tail wagging the dog.

With these changes have come problems. And baseball is facing more problems as we come to the end of this century. Among the most serious problems the game is facing, besides the increased use of drugs, are rising salaries, expansion and financially troubled franchises.

Baseball has to be careful before it expands again. It has already diluted the talent too much and that has to hurt the game. Also, there are some franchises that are in danger of going under because they can't make ends meet with the big salaries. So instead of adding new teams and making the problem worse, I think they ought to consider realigning geographically. Have an East Coast division, a Midwest division, a West Coast division. That would save money on traveling.

They are going to have to change a lot of things that they don't want to change because it's been going on for a hundred years. But they will have to change for the sake of survival.

It's like I told Lee MacPhail when, as president of the American League, he fined me. I said it's illegal. It's unconstitutional.

"You cannot fine me five hundred dollars for something I did on the field without giving me an opportunity to tell my side of the story. And you can't be judge and jury in the case. Yes, you can fine me as president of the league, but then you cannot hear my case; somebody else should be hearing it. That's what's wrong with baseball. There should be a third or fourth party sitting in and he hears the case and he has the authority to say to the league president, 'Lee MacPhail, you're wrong fining Billy Martin.'"

But Lee cannot be judge and jury.

I'm talking about the infamous Pine Tar Incident, when George Brett hit a home run that beat us in a ball game using a bat that had pine tar all the way up, almost to the top. It was too far up according to the rules, and I called that to the attention of the umpires. The umpires measured how far up the pine tar went and I was right, so they disallowed the home run.

But Dick Howser, the Kansas City manager, protested and the case went to Lee MacPhail, who overruled his own umpires and ruled that Brett's home run was legitimate. He not only ruled against the umpires, he ruled against the rules book, and he made an arbitrary decision. I had no recourse, nobody I could take my case to.

There was no question I was right. The rules

committee agreed I was right. I talked with George Sisler, president of the Columbus club in the International League and a member of the rules committee.

"Billy," Sisler told me, "you were a hundred percent right."

I talked with umpires in both leagues and they all said the same thing.

The reason the pine tar decision went against me, I believe, was that George Steinbrenner and Lee MacPhail had been fighting with each other. And I was right in the middle of the whole thing. It wasn't Billy Martin vs. The Rules. It was Lee MacPhail vs. George Steinbrenner fighting all the time, and Lee let his fight with George overshadow his good thinking and cloud his good judgment.

There's no question that the rule should have been rewritten, and it was. As it was written, it was a bad rule and an ambiguous one. But that wasn't my fault. I didn't write the rules. The way this rule was written, I was right and there was no question of that.

My argument always has been: Why make these rules if you're not going to follow them? You tell me to follow every other rule, now there comes one that I follow to the letter, and I'm right, and that one you're going to change?

Many times I will argue with an umpire and I'll tell him, "I don't give a shit if it's right or wrong; that's the rule." I didn't make the rules, but I have to comply with them and so should the umpires.

I know the rules. I read the book. Every year, before the season, I go over it again. I read it backwards, so I know what's happening out there. I know how it should be called, and if it's not, I don't have to pick up the book and turn to page forty-five to look up the rule. I already know what it says.

One of the things baseball has to do is improve the standard of umpiring. At least, it should be more consistent. What they should do is put all the umpires in a room before the season and go over what this play is, what that play is; a strict interpretation of every rule in the book, covering every possible situation. You talk to five different umpiring crews and you get five different interpretations of one thing and that's wrong.

One crew will tell me, "You're right, Billy."

Another crew, on the identical play, will say, "You're wrong, Billy."

They don't know themselves what is right and wrong, so they should get together and go over the rules and be consistent in how they call the plays.

Umpires should earn the right to be in the playoffs and World Series. They made a bad deal after their strike. Good umpires should get top salaries like a player and umpires who have a bad year—who won't hustle or are lackadaisical—should be sent down. The question is: Who is going to be the fair judge? American League umpires are as good or better than the National League. We may have one or two who need to be changed, but the NL has more.

I would even be in favor of a central umpiring system for both leagues. Let's be consistent with the strike zone, the interpretation of the rules in both leagues, so you don't have any controversy or misunderstanding or inconsistency in how a game is called or a rule interpreted when they play the All-Star Game or the World Series.

That brings me to the DH rule. I didn't like the designated hitter rule at first, for the simple reason that it took away one more decision that a manager had to make. There are managers out there that you can go for the jugular vein against because they are afraid to make decisions. You can force them to get their pitcher out of there. But with the DH, that's one less thing they have to worry about, one less decision they have to make. Without the DH, the manager has to do a little more managing. Look, it's not that difficult to adjust either way, but I have always felt that the more a manager has to think, the more decisions he has to make, the greater the advantage there is for me.

Then when the DH came in, I liked it, because you hate to see a pitcher go to the plate who can't bunt, he can't even swing the bat. Usually, the pitcher is the worst athlete on your team, so why ask him to do something he can't do?

Now I like the DH, because it puts more action in the game for the fans and I think that's what baseball has to be looking for—what's good for the fans. I think the fans want to see people do what they do best. And I think the DH puts more offense in the game.

The DH keeps big-name players around a lot longer. Don Baylor, for instance, would have a tough time playing if it wasn't for the DH. And, speaking as a fan, I would much rather see Don Baylor swing the bat than watch, say, Tommy John or Phil Niekro swing the bat.

I have no doubt that players like Joe DiMaggio, Mickey Mantle and Harmon Killebrew, Hall of Famers, would have played a few years longer if the DH rule was in effect when they were coming to the end of their careers. Reggie Jackson is another player whose career has been extended by the DH. The only thing baseball has to sell is its product: baseball games. And that means the people who play them. Shorten the careers of your big stars and you are hurting your product. That's why I am in favor of the DH, because it prolongs careers of the big-name stars, not the mediocre players.

What I don't like is for one league to have the DH and the other league not have it. Now they have changed it so that instead of having the DH in alternate years in the World Series, they are going to have it every year but use it only when the games are being played in the American League city. That's ridiculous. It still hurts the American League. What they are saying is that now, instead of having no chance, the American League has half a chance. Either throw the thing out altogether or use it in both leagues. Baseball is one sport, under one Commissioner; it should be uniform in both leagues in regard to rules and umpires.

The way it is now, I say if the National League doesn't want the DH, fine, let them play without it. They don't have to use it. But when they play the American League in the World Series, the American League will use the DH. The National League will have the option to use it or not. I'll bet you they use it. There isn't a manager who wouldn't. They don't like it, but they'll use it. So they must think there is some advantage to it.

As far as managing with or without the DH, it makes no difference. I've done it both ways. And I've won both ways. You adjust to it. Good managers can adjust to anything, but I must admit I like it without the DH, but only because I think I have an edge when a manager has more decisions to make. And you know me, I want any edge I can get.

You hear a lot of talk about speeding up the game. I agree. I don't mean it has to be "Rush, rush, rush, let's get the game over with." But you don't need eight pitches when you come in from the bullpen. The pitcher is already warmed up when he gets to the mound. He threw in the pen. He's ready when he walks in there. Or he should be. Why should he go to the mound and throw eight more pitches? Because it's been eight pitches for so many years, that's why. That's the only reason. If a pitcher comes in, two pitches and he's ready, let's go. You'll save a lot of time. Of course, he should be allowed to take as many pitches as he wants if there's an emergency and the pitcher has to come in because the first pitcher has been injured.

I don't want to make it seem like I'm knocking the game I love, that I'm biting the hand that has fed me for forty years. Baseball is still the greatest game we have, even with all its problems and its shortcomings. It has survived a hundred years and all kinds of problems —a betting coup in the 1919 World Series, drugs, free agency, expansion and long-term contracts. So it must be a great game to have survived all that. But that doesn't mean it can't be even better. No matter how good a thing is, or a person is, there is always room for improvement.

23

My supporters have said I am one of the best managers in the history of baseball.

My critics grudgingly say I may be all right for a year or two, but sooner or later you have to pay the price.

What do I think?

People talk about the bottom line. All right, let's look at the bottom line.

Does Billy Martin win? Yeah, Billy Martin wins.

Do the people fill the stadium? Yeah, the people fill the stadium.

Does he give all of himself? Yeah, he gives all of himself.

I'm the only manager in the history of baseball who took two teams that lost 100 games in one year and made them successful the next year. Look it up. In 1973, the Texas Rangers lost 105 games. I got there for the last 23 games. The following year, we finished second in the American League West with a record of 84–76.

In 1979, the Oakland A's lost 108 games. The following year we finished second in the American League West with a record of 83–79.

What do they want? They want me to manage the way they want and lose? I can't do that. When I manage, I have to manage Billy Martin's way. I have to live and die on my own convictions. If I have to go down the drain, I've got to be able to say it was my fault. I lost. I can't blame the third base coach, I can't blame the pitchers, I can't blame the hitters. I can't blame the owner. It was my fault. I didn't win.

People are always looking for excuses to justify their decisions. Baseball does that. When I first started managing in Denver, they said: "How can he manage a baseball team when he can't even manage himself?"

The next year it was: "He's a hothead. He can't control himself and he can't control players."

Then: "He drinks too much."

Every year they try to find something that I do wrong, something to put me down, to discredit me. Something to tarnish my record. But the record speaks for itself.

As a manger, I have had my share of Most Valuable Players and a bunch of 20-game winners. Wherever I have gone, teams improve and individual performances improve. Do you think that's a coincidence?

In Minnesota, I had Harmon Killebrew and he

won the Most Valuable Player award as a third base-man. Then I went to Texas and I had another MVP, Jeff Burroughs. In fact, in 1974, we swept it all—Burroughs, MVP; Mike Hargrove, Rookie of the Year; and I was Manager of the Year.

In New York, I had another Most Valuable Player in 1976, Thurman Munson, and another in 1985, Don Mattingly.

Whenever a team is going down the drain and they need somebody to save it, who do they call? Billy Martin, that's who. I've saved two franchises already.

I think they ought to take a look at my record and say, "Look, he did it with five different clubs, not just one like Tommy Lasorda and Earl Weaver. Or like Sparky Anderson, who won with a great team in Cincinnati and a good one in Detroit. Look at the teams he did it with, then measure the man as a manager."

That's the true measure of a manager. Not his record alone, but how he improved teams that others failed with. And how those teams went down the drain after he left.

Leonard Koppett, the sportswriter, is one of the most knowledgeable people around, a thinking man's baseball writer. He goes beneath the surface and studies figures and trends. He doesn't just give statistics, he tries to explain reasons why certain things happen.

In a recent article, Koppett pointed out that when I was in Oakland, I and my coaching staff had been involved with twenty teams in our careers that finished first. "Winning experiences," Koppett called them. He explained that if my pitching coach, Art Fowler, and I had been together with Detroit when we won our division, that would count for only one winning experience. And we had twenty such winning experiences among the manager and coaches.

After I left Oakland, they had a coaching staff and manager in 1986 who had a total of only one winning experience among them. And, Koppett pointed out, that one was when they coached for me in Oakland.

Koppett then came to this conclusion:

"People he works for look at how easily, efficiently and quickly Billy seems to turn losers into winners and they say, 'I can do that.' So they fire him, thinking they can do the same thing, and, of course, they can't."

They ask you to lead and to be a manager, then when you try to do it, the owners don't back you. That's the part that makes me mad. They'll say all along: "Billy, you have to do this, you have to do that, you have to be strict." Then when you're strict, they say you're too strict.

Or they say you're too close to the players. Or you're not close enough to the players, you don't communicate with them.

How many excuses are there?

Whatever suits their convenience at the time they're firing me. They hire you because you're a battler, because you're a competitor, because you're fiery and feisty. They even use these words in their press release announcing you as the new manager: "fiery Billy Martin, the feisty," etc.

Then once they hire you, they try to change you. I don't get it.

It's like a marriage. A woman says, "I love you, honey," then once she gets the ring and the wedding certificate, she wants to change all your habits. She wants to make you into the man she wants you to be, not the man you were when she met you and fell in love with you. And pretty soon, you're divorced. Why are you divorced? Because she wouldn't let you be you. She won't let you be the person you were when she met you.

As this is being written, and maybe as it is being read, I am not managing a baseball team. I think that's a terrible waste of my life, of my talent. That's like Frank Sinatra not singing or Robert De Niro not acting or Michelangelo not painting.

I'm not looking for a job. I'm working for the New York Yankees in television and public relations and as a consultant and I'm very happy doing what I'm doing. George Steinbrenner has given me a lifetime job with the Yankees and I appreciate it.

Would I manage again?

To be honest, I'd have to say, "Yes, I would." I'd like to show somebody just one more time that I can do it, that I can win.

But I don't want to go just anyplace to manage just for the sake of managing. It has to be right. I'm proud to be a Yankee and I'm happy working for the Yankees. Unless it's right, I'm not going to leave the Yankees. I'm a Yankee.

During the 1986 season, there were rumors flying around that I was going to manage this club, I was going to manage that club. Mainly, the rumors centered on the Chicago White Sox, the Minnesota Twins and the Yankees. This is the truth about that.

The White Sox contacted me. That is, Ken "Hawk" Harrelson, their general manager and an old friend, contacted my lawyer, Eddie Sapir. Eddie and I talked about it, and Eddie talked with Harrelson, and there was one meeting between me and Hawk.

We told Harrelson what it would take to get me to manage, and I didn't come cheap. Hawk listened, but said nothing. And he never offered me the job. I don't know if it was that I overpriced myself or that he had second thoughts about me. All I know is that he never got back to me, and the next thing I knew, they had named Jim Fregosi as manager. No hard feelings. I wish them well.

Fregosi left the Louisville club, a St. Louis Cardinals' farm in the American Association, to take the White Sox job. Louisville is owned by A. Ray Smith, who runs a great operation. The Louisville club draws around one million people every year. It often outdraws some major league teams. When he lost Fregosi, A. Ray Smith called me and asked me to take over his club for the balance of the season. He was going to pay me $150,000 for half a season.

I must admit it was a generous offer and I was tempted. The reason I was tempted is that I wanted to help out A. Ray. But I also had a commitment to George Steinbrenner and television station WPIX, and I didn't think it made any sense for me to leave New York to go to the minor leagues. So I told A. Ray I appreciated his offer, but I had to decline.

As for the rumors that I was going to manage the Minnesota Twins or that I was going to replace Lou Piniella as manager of the Yankees, that's all they were, rumors.

I had no conversations with any member of the Twins organization about managing that club, and neither did Eddie Sapir. The way that rumor got started, a couple of newspaper guys wrote that I would be the right man to replace Ray Miller and put the Twins back into contention. They even supported that by telling the same thing to Carl Pohlad, the man who bought the Twins from Calvin Griffith. But that's as far as it went. Nobody from the Twins ever contacted me, I was never interviewed for the job, and I never contacted them.

Also, there were no conversations between George Steinbrenner and me, or between George and Eddie Sapir, about my replacing Piniella as manager of the Yankees. Those were just rumors with no basis in fact.

On the contrary, publicly, on my television broadcasts, and privately, speaking with friends, I praised Piniella for the job he did under difficult circumstances and said I thought Lou deserved the chance to come back in 1987. I even urged Steinbrenner to rehire Piniella. And I couldn't be happier to see that Lou will be back.

If I ever took another managing job, it would have to be right. I would like to work for somebody who really appreciates what I do out there, somebody who appreciates that I put my heart into it when I manage and that I'm not the Billy Martin they read about.

I guess that's the one thing that bothers me the most, the one thing about my life that I would change if I could. I'd like to be remembered as me, how I am, how I *really* am. But that will never happen, I'm afraid.

I guess I'm destined to be remembered as Billy the Kid in baseball, a quick shooter, a battler. I don't like that. What I would like is to be remembered by the people who know me best.

Late in the 1985 season, I got this note from my old teammate Bobby Brown, president of the American League. It was dated September 21. I'd like to share it with you.

Dear Billy,
I wanted to write you and tell you I think you have done an outstanding job with the Yan-

kees. I know you are having your troubles now but that doesn't in the least detract from the excellent way you have handled the team since you took over. Everyone that knows anything about baseball shares my sentiments.

I hope health wise you get to feeling better —I will visit with you before the season's end.

Sincerely,
Bobby

That's the kind of thing that means so much to me, that a man as busy as Bobby Brown took the time and the trouble to write and that he appreciates what I do and what I am.

The best thing about my forty years in baseball has been the wonderful people I have met, the great friends I have made. I have talked about some of them —my teammates Joe DiMaggio, Mickey Mantle, Yogi Berra and Whitey Ford; Casey Stengel and Charlie Dressen. So many, many people who have been close to me that it would take this whole book to list them all. And then I'd probably forget someone and that would make him mad at me.

I would, however, like to make mention of one individual who has meant so much to me from the first day I showed up in spring training with the Yankees. In fact, he was the first person I met when I became a Yankee.

That would be Pete Sheehy, the longtime equipment manager of the Yankees, who remained very special to me from that day in 1950 when I first walked into training camp until his death in 1985. Pete was just a wonderful, beautiful, thoughtful man. I really loved him. That's why it hurt me so much when George Steinbrenner wanted me to have a team workout on the day Pete was laid out in the funeral parlor. That hurt me more than anything else, but George just couldn't understand that.

I was really close to Pete. I was only twenty years old when I came up to the Yankees and Pete took care of me like I was his own son. He'd tell me how to act in the clubhouse, what I should do, what I shouldn't do. He cautioned me to watch what I said. He and Joe DiMaggio were the ones who looked after me when I came to the Yankees.

I guess Pete took a liking to me because he was always for the underdog and I was an underdog. He was on my bandwagon from the first day I got to camp.

It was Pete Sheehy who gave me my No. 1. As equipment manager, it was up to Pete to assign numbers to players, and when I got there, George Stirnweiss had No. 1. Pete gave me No. 12. Later, Stirnweiss was traded, but Pete wouldn't give out his number to anyone, and when I went into the Army, Pete saved the number for me.

"Nobody's going to get that number," Pete would say when people asked him about it. "That's Billy's number."

And he gave me No. 1 when I got out of the Army and told me I got that number because my back wasn't broad enough for two numbers. But I knew different.

Later, when I was managing against the Yankees for the Twins, Tigers, Rangers and A's and I would come into Yankee Stadium as the manager of the visiting team, Pete would never fail to come over to the visiting manager's office to say hello.

When I returned to the Yankees in 1975, it was a little strange because Yankee Stadium was being renovated and we were playing our home games in Shea

Stadium, where the Mets play. That kind of took a little away from going back to the Yankees, but when I walked into the clubhouse that first day and saw Pete Sheehy, I knew I had come home.

Pete never said anything about my return. He just hugged me and welcomed me back, but I could tell from the look in his eyes what he was feeling. And the feeling was mutual.

I was no longer a twenty-year-old rookie who didn't know his way around, but Pete still looked after me. He'd never fail to come to me on Saturday night, or Sunday morning, to remind me that church services were starting in a few minutes and he'd see that I went with him.

About a month before Pete died, I asked a photographer, Louie Requena, to take a picture of me and Pete. When Louie developed the picture, I asked Pete to sign it. He did. This is what he wrote:

"To Billy: You'll always be No. 1 with me. Pete Sheehy."

I still have the picture. I cherish it, just as I cherish the memory and friendship of Pete Sheehy, who will always be No. 1 with me.

I want to take this opportunity to thank you, the fans, who have been so supportive of me, who have written me letters with your good wishes. I appreciate them. Every one of them. I wish I could tell each of you thanks in person, or could have written to each one of you, but time would not permit. So let this suffice. Thanks.

Maybe you won't see me in uniform again managing some team. If not, it has been a hell of a run and a great privilege for me to have done what I have done for a living, to have spent most of my life in the game I love so much and for the New York Yankees, the team I love so much.

Will I ever manage again?

I wouldn't bet against it. Would you?